BLACK☆AND☆BLUE

Understanding Modern Law Enforcement In Your America

Derwin J. Bradley

Bloomington, IN   Milton Keynes, UK

AuthorHouse™
1663 Liberty Drive, Suite 200
Bloomington, IN 47403
www.authorhouse.com
Phone: 1-800-839-8640

AuthorHouse™ UK Ltd.
500 Avebury Boulevard
Central Milton Keynes, MK9 2BE
www.authorhouse.co.uk
Phone: 08001974150

First published by AuthorHouse 1/25/2007

ISBN: 978-1-4259-8784-8 (sc)

Printed in the United States of America
Bloomington, Indiana

This book is printed on acid-free paper.

OPEN TO SUGGESTION. None is so perfect that he may not at times need a monitor, for he is incurably the fool who will not listen. Even the most high should lend ear to friendly advice, for sovereignty itself may not shut off gentlemanly counsel. There are men who cannot be saved because they cannot be reached, who hurl themselves to destruction because none dares approach to restrain them. The most faultless should leave open one door to friendship, for it may prove a portal of succor. Place should be made for one friend at least to advise without embarrassment, even to find fault; but this privilege should rest upon his rightness, upon our trust in him, and his understanding…

-Baltasar Gracian

In The Beginning...

This project originally began as a rebuttal to the information and recommendations on Fostering Accountable Community Centered Policing that was presented in The Covenant with Black America. I (and others that read it) felt that inflammatory and misleading information was being offered to African-Americans as gospel (again) and that it was time for some hard truths to be told to set the record straight.

However, as the book progressed, it occurred to me that it wasn't just Blacks that didn't understand American Law Enforcement. The more I dug into my memory banks for stories; I realized that most Americans were absolutely clueless as to what real Law Enforcement is and how Law Enforcement Officials go about doing their jobs. In your defense good citizens, I do recognize that the majority of you get your ideas about police work by watching television or movies, and therein lies most of the problem.

So even though the tone of this book is set for African-Americans, it really does apply to all of you out there in your own little America, and even to those of you in other countries that have modern police forces.

In this book you will not see a whole lot of statistical data thrown at you. If you want statistics, go online and simply Google whatever information you're seeking. I promise you that you'll find more statistical data than you can handle!

What I'm going to share with you is real life. I'm offering a quick view of real police work from real police officers and it should help you in your quest to better understand American Law Enforcement. Only then can you start building better relationships with your respective Law Enforcement Agencies, if that is your goal. Or, you can simply read this book and enjoy it for its entertainment value. It's your choice.

Now, I'll say to you what I tell people on the street when they are about to make an unwise choice during an encounter with the police. This ain't no movie, and it ain't no television show, this is real life and it is happening to you *right now!*

CONTENTS

SECTION I – AMERICAN LEO-101

"Of the troops, for the troops"

-US ARMY MILITARY POLICE MOTTO

Just as it is in the military, it is in civilian life. The police are the community, and they are here for the community. Unfortunately, police officers are still an enigma in our society. People tend to adhere to old stereotypes or incorrect conclusions drawn from watching television police shows or action movies. In many cases, citizens get their information about police officers from criminals, which will obviously be a little skewed. Many citizens think that they can watch an episode of CSI and know the inner workings of police investigations. While it is true that some shows portray real-life cases, they hardly scratch the surface of what real police officers do or how they behave. So, in most cases what you think you know about police and police work will be wrong. Let's see what I can do to help change that.

But before we get into the heavy stuff, I'm going to give you a quick overview of American law enforcement agencies and the men and women that staff them.

Municipal Police Departments (more commonly known as City Police)-
Responsible for Law Enforcement within incorporated areas or city limits. A municipal police department is typically led by the Chief of Police. The Chief of Police is usually appointed by the Mayor, the City Manager, or City Council. City Police officers are typically unionized and have civil service protection.

County Sheriff- Sheriff's Departments-
Generally considered the most powerful of local law enforcement agencies because their area of responsibility usually cover an entire county, which sometimes encompasses several cities or municipalities. The Sheriff is elected by the people and can only be removed from office by the Governor, and then only under extreme circumstances. Sheriff's deputies serve at his or her pleasure and generally don't have civil service protection. Most Sheriffs also control the county jails.

State Police (sometimes known as Highway Patrol Officers or State Troopers)-

Responsible for enforcement of laws on roads and highways outside of the city limits. Their jurisdiction is statewide. They also secure the state capital and provide security for the governor.

Federal Agents- Enforce federal laws only. They generally do not have local enforcement powers.

Prison/Jail Officials- Prisons are run by Federal, State, and County agencies. Jurisdiction is typically limited to prison/jail facilities.

Here's a little known fact: the titles of police officer, deputy sheriff, or state trooper is given to an employee by the agency that hires him or her. All police officers, deputies, and troopers are trained and certified by the state and are officially designated as Law Enforcement Officials-hence the acronym, LEO.

The LEO takes an oath and is sworn to uphold the laws created by local, state and federal governments. However, you should know that law enforcement agencies do not make the laws- they just enforce them!

Laws are created by state legislators, city councils, and county commissions, so if you encounter a law that you think is trivial or specifically targets Black people, take it up with them.

Law enforcement is commonly recognized as the most efficient component of the criminal justice system because we tend to catch the criminals faster than they can be processed through the rest of the system. Law enforcement is a serious, dangerous and often violent business but thanks to the brave men and women who have chosen to become law enforcement officials, the criminals are brought to justice.

But are officers perfect? No. Do they make mistakes? Yes. Do they bring to work their life's experiences, instincts, prejudices, and biases? Yes they do. Just like every judge, janitor, attorney, senator, car salesman, doctor, movie theater employee, and fast food worker, the LEO brings everything that makes them who they are to work. Get the point? Everyone that is able to come out and work among other human beings bring all of their personal baggage with them. Like I said before, this ain't no movie, this is real life! Police officers are human too!

When you work in the world of law enforcement, you get to experience the very worst of what society has to offer in the way of abhorrent human behavior. The sad truth is that average American citizen lie so much about the crimes that they are involved in that police just don't believe anything that they say. We see violent offender commit a heinous crime, leave a ton of evidence behind, and still stand before a court and plead not guilty! We see so-called upstanding citizens lie about causing a simple vehicle crash, and then throw a hissy-fit if they get a ticket. People lie about shoplifting, even though they were seen and recorded on camera committing the crime. I have arrested countless 'innocent' people on warrants who usually swear that it's not them right up until the time we get to the jail and then suddenly their memory returns and they remember what they did to get in trouble in the first place. Whites lie, Blacks lie, Hispanics lie, Asians lie, professionals lie, homeless people lie, everyone lies to the police! They lie to be right, they lie to justify illegal behavior, and the number one reason they lie is to escape punishment. So by the time we retire or leave the profession, our faith in humanity is shot. We often don't trust anyone outside our family, co-workers, and circle of friends.

Don't get me wrong, we do care about you. We'll be the first ones to risk our lives for any one of you without a moment's hesitation. Yes we'll do it even if we don't particularly care for you!

For example: One night I was chasing a drug dealer who we knew had a warrant outstanding for his arrest. I cornered him in an alley and he immediately went for his gun. Fortunately, I was faster on the draw that night and won the confrontation. Nearly two years later, my partner and I rescued that very same drug dealer from several other dealers who were trying to kill him. Was he one of my favorite people? No. Could I have left him to die? Yes, but that would have been morally, professionally, and legally wrong.

What I'm trying to say is that even though we may not particularly care for an individual for whatever reason, we will still put it on the line to help him.

Here's another thing that you may not know about the police, sometimes you all really get on our nerves! Don't get angry! This is simply more proof that police are human! Back in the eighties I read a magazine article titled, "Why Cops Hate You! If you have to ask, get out of the way!" To be perfectly honest it was absolutely hilarious, and so very true! The author wrote about how stupid and clueless people can be and how the get themselves into terrible situations by walking blindly into danger! They don't believe that anything bad will happen to them because, well, this is just like the movies!

For instance, if you see wide-eyed officers running around with rifles, shotguns, and pistols drawn, you should probably seek cover! But you don't! Instead you waltz right to the officer and ask, "Officer is everything okay?" Or, "Officer is it safe?" Or my personal favorite, "Officer am I in any danger?" You can imagine the answers that run through our minds as we strain to maintain our professional composure. You see, not only do we have to keep track of the armed suspect or suspects, we now have to protect the curious citizen or group of citizens that have wandered into the combat zone. A smack upside the head is now probably in order but that would be counterproductive to one's career, as would be a string of stinging expletives! So instead we give a strained, "Get back inside!" through our teeth and quickly move away from them.

Not quite what you expected to hear is it? What? You thought that you knew all about police officers because you watched Bad Boys or CSI? Or did you think that you could pick up a copy of The Covenant with Black America, read a few lines of statistical data, theory, and propaganda written by a non-law enforcement source, and you would have the magic key on how to deal with modern American law enforcement? No such luck folks. While I'm sure the authors in the Covenant meant well, quoting vague statistical data and playing on old fears just won't get you where you need to be in enjoying a good working relationship with your local law enforcement agency.

You see, you can force the agency managers to bend to your will because politicians and administrators all want positive press, but to get the first responders- the officers on the street to appreciate your point of view, you must first get to know them a little better. Please empty your cup (that is, let go of what you think you know) for me. I need your minds open and ready for some serious information because you need to know what's really happening out here on the streets. Most of all, I need you to wake up from the past and join the rest of us here in the present, so that you'll be ready for a powerful new future! Get in, let's go for a ride.

SECTION II- AMBUSHED!

"Never accuse others to excuse yourself"

-ANONYMOUS

In May of 2006, at about 1:00 am, a thirty-year-old Black attorney was driving through a Black neighborhood on the way to his mother's house. Traveling in the opposite direction was a rookie police officer that noticed a headlight out on the approaching vehicle. Naturally, the young officer decided to stop the vehicle.

The officer approached the vehicle and asked the young attorney for his license and registration. The young man asked the officer why he was being stopped. In keeping with standard practice, the officer did not answer and again asked for the driver license and registration. The young attorney then called his mother and told her that he was being profiled. Now this is not unusual. Citizens often seek comfort from a friend or family member during a traffic encounter with the police. It is a stressful event because no one, and I mean Blacks, American Indian, Hispanics, Asians, and yes, even White people like to be stopped by the police!

Unfortunately for the young officer, the driver of the Volvo that he had just stopped was the son of a City Commissioner.

The young attorney had several options at this point; he could have dropped his mother's name and gotten out of the ticket. Or he could have 'manned up' and taken the $75.00 ticket, which would have been reduced to something like $11.50 if he had gotten it fixed and brought the car to the police station to be inspected. He chose to do neither. Instead, he kept his window rolled up and called his mommy and told her that he was being racially profiled by a White officer and was afraid that he might get shot or Tased by the obviously racist officer.

How fortunate for the young attorney that he was dealing with a rookie officer. A seasoned officer would have given him a chance to roll down the window, then forcibly removed him from the car and arrested him. But I'm glad things happened the way they did because the following chain of events led to this effort to properly educate you on how to handle yourself during a police encounter.

Well, as expected, mommy called the chief at home (remember, it's about 1:00 am) and began screaming at him to do something. Naturally, the chief called the watch commander and asked him to look into it. The watch commander and the sergeant responded to the scene and sent the young attorney on his way. The sergeant had the officer mail the citation to the attorney the next day.

Somehow, the media got wind of the incident and the young attorney began screaming racial profiling to anyone that would listen. It just so happens that the young man was running for a seat on the county commission at the time of incident. How convenient. He joyfully basked in the media attention that his unjust cause had begun to generate.

The would-be commissioner's mother was quoted in the paper as saying, "I didn't want some White boy shooting my son!" The law enforcement community was shocked, but I wasn't. I've heard this Commissioner use racial slurs on several occasions when referring to White people. (Yes, Black people can be racist too).

The police had backed this particular commissioner during her election so the sting was most painful.

However, I was furious at the young attorney. Not only was he attempting to smear the agency's good reputation and create racial tension where there was none, his whiny, sniveling, mama's-boy actions set Black men in this city back at least twenty years!

For the next couple of weeks I watched this sad affair on television and in the paper as the young man garnered sympathy from the uneducated, the enablers, and of course, from the local criminal element. Fortunately, most of the city criticized him (and his mommy) because they saw him for what he was, a snot-nosed mama's boy who attempted to trash the reputation of a top-notch agency just so he could get some publicity for his campaign for county commissioner.

I desperately wanted to meet him face to face and tell him what a loser he was and to get his mommy's tit out of his mouth and 'man up'! Actually, it was the Black women that I interviewed that actually suggested the removal of the breast from his mouth. They also asked the same question that I had in mind. Is this the type of man we want as a community leader?

White officers who I interviewed asked, "Weren't her comments racist?" Of course they knew that the comments were unwarranted and racist, but White men don't dare say such things in public, especially to a Black co-worker, lest they are labeled a racist and written up.

Look readers- if the young attorney thought that he was being racially profiled, he should have at least waited until the officer completed the encounter before he went crying to mommy. Later, I'm going to tell you exactly how to tell if you've been racially profiled and what to do about it.

The media circus continued and the more he whined and she cursed, the angrier I got. The commissioner began attacking the police department and called for the resignation of the chief of police. The community rallied behind the agency and called for the commissioner to resign. It was one really ugly situation!

The following week, my associate pastor called and asked me if I would sit on a panel at the church and discuss the Covenant with Black America and in particular, the section on Fostering Accountable Community-Centered Policing. I quickly agreed because I was aware that the community would be unnecessarily enraged because of recent events. I thanked God for the opportunity to set the record straight and tell the community the truth about how the Department does business. I wanted them to know that the agency did not have problem with racial profiling. I'm not saying that it doesn't happen; I'm saying that our agency rarely experiences it from our officers. Besides, if I knew that my agency openly practiced or endorsed any type of racist policing policies, I would not speak for them and they know that!

The pastor told me to be prepared to respond to questions from church members about what my agency was doing to foster good relations with the public. I might also mention that I later learned that this event was planned long before the infamous traffic stop.

I was very excited about the upcoming event. I spent five years in the community relations section and was also a commissioner's liaison so I loved educating the public about the police department. I was also excited about reading The Covenant in hopes of seeing some groundbreaking advice and guidance for Blacks in America. Then I began reading section four of The Covenant with Black America, Fostering Accountable Community-Centered Policing.

My stomach churned as I struggled to digest and comprehend what I was reading. I was shocked! This is what they're selling as truth and recommending to Black America as a way to work with law enforcement?

Not that all of the recommendations were bad, but it was quite obvious that they were conceived by someone who has no expertise in law enforcement and the recommendations are a little, well, unrealistic.

The main thing I found to be misleading was the way the statistical data and essays were presented. It's basically saying that most police hate you because you're Black and they're out to get you. So now they've either scared the crap out people or they've really pissed them off and then offered only theoretical solutions that have no flavor or substance. They played on the emotions of readers and got everyone all fired up and angered them against the very people that they were supposed to be learning how to get along with. Now if that was not the author's intentions, I stand corrected. Maybe my anger stems from the really bad presentation of the information. At any rate, I shall press on and endeavor to give you solid information that will give you all of the tools and realistic information that you will need to have a better relationship with your local law enforcement agency.

As I read the introductory essay of chapter four of the Covenant, I knew that it would send the wrong message to Black people. The Covenant author made reference to a frightening Rap video that she had seen. I recall seeing that same video depicting Blacks in a concentration camp, surrounded by armed White guards with snarling police dogs, barbed-wired fences, and spotlights. I however, understood it for what it was: garbage! It was an obviously successful media ploy designed to inflame emotions and sell albums. In other words, it was Rap propaganda. I also find it difficult to give validity to a rapper's point of view, particularly when most rap encourages misogyny, drug and alcohol abuse, idolizing money, and the wholesale, ruthless slaughter of Black males.

Then, the author offers statistics to make you believe that there is a real danger of Blacks being thrown into a Nazi-style concentration camp. Talk about fear mongering!

Yes the numbers are real. There are a lot of Black men in prisons and jails around the country. However, the author left out some critical statistical data. Those people are actually committing crimes! Yes, I know it is hard to believe, but Black men are committing crimes, and lots of them!

Now for those of you who sit on the sidelines and cry foul, I invite you to go to your local police agency and look at the calls for service. Ask to see the event log, which outlines mostly felony crimes in your community. Read some of the reports and witness for yourself what's going on in your community. Or just go to a high-crime area (you know where they are), and see it first hand if you dare.

For now, stay with me and I'll enlighten you a little.

If you've read section four of 'The Covenant', you'll notice I am loosely following its format so that it will be easy reading for you. For the rest of you, I'll rewrite some of the author's remarks so that you will be up to speed on the topic.

I'm going to hit you with a cold, hard fact that you may not be aware of. America has racism in it! Yes, there are actually people here who don't like Black people! I know it's a shock, but try to maintain. Here's a little known fact. America is the fundraising hub for White supremacy groups around the world. Now you know! Now I'll ask Black Americans an important question. Do you think that you would be safer in Africa? How about Jamaica or Haiti? Think about that as we move along. (By the way, I've been to Africa and most of you wouldn't last a week).

Moving right along…. Now that you know that there is racism in America and that there is racial bias in our criminal justice system, conduct yourselves accordingly! Stay out of trouble! Don't commit crimes!

I know that I make it sound incredibly simplistic, but that simple formula has worked for me, as well as millions of other Blacks in this country!

Those of us who know better know that any solution to the growing crisis of mass Black incarceration must begin with the focus of not how our communities or youth are policed, but how our communities and youth conduct themselves. You see, if you want responsible policing, you must be responsible citizens. It is every person's duty to help maintain an orderly society by conducting themselves in a civilized manner. That means obeying the laws of the land and helping the police to keep your neighborhood safe.

This is a direct comment from some of the White officers who I interviewed, "We just want them (Blacks), to be responsible for their own communities." Some Black officers say this also, but neither group will say it in mixed company.

The Covenant author is right when she says that the police are the enforcers of society. They have the authority, the duty, and the mission to enforce the laws of the land. Yes they make decisions about who to target and how. That is exactly what the police are supposed to do. I don't agree with the author when she says that the DECISIONS ARE OFTEN RACE-BASED. I disagree because it makes it sound as if the police are hunting Black people. The reality is that the targeting is done based on the community that the officer works in. It is the racial makeup of a particular neighborhood that determines who the police encounter, and it is usually the people that live in that particular community.

That, my friends, comes not from a distant researcher, but from someone who has had boots on ground in all types of communities. Don't you think that it's time that we stop assuming and get the facts? The fact is, you don't really know what the police do other communities because you don't live in those communities! I know that may not sit well with a lot of you, but it is the simple truth. Let's get into this!

SECTION III-CULTURAL SENSITIVITY

"Comprehension is not a prerequisite for compliance"

-Councilman in THE MATRIX: REVOLUTIONS

I remember when we all had to go through cultural diversity training at our agency. Race relations were tense and emotions wore very thin. White officers felt as if they were being singled out and their attitudes reflected that thought process. Blacks and Latinos felt that they didn't need to change because they were the minorities and their attitudes reflected that thought process. The truth of the matter was that we all had some cultural growing to do.

I learned something very sobering during that period of departmental readjustment. I learned that no training, or policy, or order can make someone like or even respect someone else. I realized that only strict, consistent, and fairly enforced rules of conduct could ensure the proper treatment of citizens when they have encounters with the police.

If an officer of a certain race or gender doesn't like a citizen of a certain race or gender, there is nothing that the agency can do about it. They can only control the officer's professional conduct, not his or her feelings, emotions, and prejudices. The agency cannot force an officer to be nice to the public. They can only force the officer to be courteous and professional. I work with a lot of officers who are professional and efficient, but have zero personality so they come across cold and rude. There is not much an agency can do about that type of officer as long as he or she doesn't violate policy and procedure.

Police officers are constantly reminded that they are held to a 'higher standard' than the public both on and off duty. Our behavior in our private lives is as closely monitored as our behavior at work. So if a citizen saw me off duty doing or saying something that is considered 'conduct unbecoming an officer' they could report me to the department and an official internal inquiry would be initiated.

I recently saw in the news where a police agency was forced to rehire an officer who is an avowed racist and member of a well-known White supremacy group, so I guess times are changing. Even the military is now keeping soldiers who are documented and active members in hate groups. How much do you think those types of people are going to care about you and your culture?

I've noticed that citizens get very upset if 'officer friendly' does not smile when they arrive on a scene.

Please try and remember that law enforcement is a dangerous and serious profession. Don't take it personal because we may have just left a scene where someone was killed or we could have just been in a big fight. (No we don't get to go home after a violent confrontation.) We are not here to entertain you, and our job is nothing like the movies or those corny television police shows.

Case in point: While on patrol late one night, I was driving past a nightclub and someone took a shot at me! The bullet hit the top of the car door just above my head! We caught the shooter after a short chase and locked him up. The following night the sergeant wanted to have a civilian from the Citizen's Review Board ride with me for a shift. I was still furious about being shot at and should not have even been at work, but they wouldn't let me take the night off. I asked the sergeant to put her with someone else but she insisted that the woman ride with me. It was a horrible experience for both of us. I don't think that I said two words to the poor lady and she complained on me afterwards. The department has since improved its policy in dealing with officers involved in critical stress incidents such as officer-involved shootings and similar situations.

Most Americans believe that the police are here to protect and serve. That's not entirely true. The title of police officer, deputy sheriff, or state trooper, are all given by the agency that hires the individual for that particular job. As I mentioned earlier, the official title for the people employed in those jobs is Law Enforcement Official, or LEO. That is the title given by state or federal lawmakers who grant the LEO the authority to act on the government and society's behalf when they enforce the laws set forth by said lawmakers. In other words, the LEO is really here to keep you, the citizen, in line.

Now given the seriousness of that daunting responsibility, it is very difficult for the average officer to go about his or her busy day, be professional in terrifying situations, stay alive, and try to care deeply about a stranger's cultural differences. In virtually no other profession is this monitored more, and rightfully so. Now I'm not saying that the officer shouldn't try to be sensitive, I'm just saying that sometimes it is difficult to handhold the public at times. There are a few officers that can easily soothe citizens and cross cultures with ease and savvy, but not many. That's just the way it is folks and the more you push cultural sensitivity, the more resistance you're going to get. More than any other profession, police officers adapt to the surroundings in which they work. If the dominant populace is violent and apathetic, then the police will treat them as such. The same applies with a calm and caring populace. In other words, the officers will treat you the way you behave.

I've worked in both types of neighborhoods and believe me when I tell you that few officers excel in transitioning between the two and I guarantee that most of you couldn't do it either. The majority of you reading this book are no more adept at being culturally sensitive than the officer that will respond to your call for assistance. Furthermore, I can almost guarantee that the officer has had more training and experience in dealing with diverse cultures than you have had.

The bottom line is that law enforcement is an emotionally tough job so many officers learn to turn their emotions off or risk a nervous breakdown. Its not that officers don't care; it's just that they can't afford to get emotionally involved in their work- the price is simply too high. All that being said, the officer must still comply with department regulations with regard to respecting the various cultures in our communities. The officer may not understand or even care about a different culture, but in the end he or she will comply or risk disciplinary action.

SECTION IV-RACIAL PROFILING

"It is only with the heart that one can see rightly; what is essential is invisible to the eye."

-ANTOINE DE SAINT-EXUPERY

Racial profiling was really bad during the late eighties and early nineties when crack cocaine hit the scene. Drug dealers invented ingenious ways of transporting their product and at one point in time were moving hundreds of millions of dollars along our nation's highways. The police quickly caught on and developed a strategy for targeting transporters of illegal narcotics. The profiling actually worked well, but unfortunately, many officers got stuck in a pattern and unlawfully stopped and detained innocent Black motorists. I even heard of a few cases where large sums of money were taken for no reason!

My own personal experience happened as I traveled South on I75 through Macon, Georgia. A Georgia State Trooper with Canine pulled me over one fine afternoon as I was returning from Atlanta. Luckily I wasn't speeding at the time, so I knew that he had profiled me. I rolled down my window, put my hands on the steering wheel, and waited. The Trooper called for me to step out of the car. I turned the vehicle off, got out, and pressed the button to lock the vehicle. I waited in silence as he explained to me that he stopped me because my window tint was too dark. I calmly informed him that the tint was factory installed. I smiled at him and folded my arms. He half-smiled, stuttered a bit and said that the frame around my license plate was illegal in Georgia. I pointed to the license plate and reminded him that I was from Florida and that I was merely passing through. He smiled openly now, knowing that I had him beat. He made small talk for a moment then sent me on my way. I never told him that I was a policeman because I wanted to see if he would try and search my vehicle. I wasn't going to let him, but I did want to see if he would try. I knew that I had been profiled. He saw a Black male driving in a late model SUV and decided to give it a shot. I didn't lose my cool during or even after the incident (and I certainly didn't call my mommy!).

So you see I agree with statistical data and studies because a lot of police agencies profiled Blacks on the Interstate at the height of the drug war. (My agency was not allowed to participate in those operations).

However, the Covenant author also mentioned that police look for drugs primarily in Black communities and that a large number of Blacks are arrested, prosecuted, convicted, and incarcerated. Here's a news flash: it's got nothing to do with racial profiling. It was another attempt to get you upset and cloud your thinking! Let's set the record straight.

The night of the meeting at my church, the commissioner whose son cried racial profiling arrived with her police liaison. I had forgotten that she was a member of my church. (I don't ever recall seeing her there.)

I knew right away that this was going to be a show! Every television, radio, and print media crew was on the scene. I then spotted the young attorney. I figured that he would grill us from the audience and try to score some points on camera. I was wrong. When the panel went up on stage, he came right up and sat next to me! I couldn't have prayed for a better opportunity.

The Patrol operations bureau chief, a retired officer, and I gave stellar performances, and destroyed any hopes the young attorney had of humiliating us. He stuttered through his presentation, quoting vague statistical data, quoted the Covenant author and spoke of the police arresting Blacks in drug sweeps. When the crowd didn't respond to him, he went off on a tangent about how South American Cartels grow and provide drugs to America, then White men ship the drugs into America and that Black men don't own any boats or planes. Then magically, the drugs are dropped into Black communities and Blacks somehow ended up in prison! It would have been funny if it weren't so pathetic. I had been hearing that same lame story from Black for almost twenty years now. I couldn't take it; I had to set him straight.

After the meeting, I pulled him aside. I agreed with him that the cartels send the drugs in via wealthy White or Hispanic men with boats. (I'm sure we all know that Blacks do own ships and planes). Then I broke it down for him. I told him that the truth of the matter is that White people typically will not tolerate open-air drug sales in their communities. So the White men use mid-level Black managers to distribute the drugs to low-level Black, street dealers, who in turn stand on the corners of Black neighborhoods and sell dope to anyone that comes their way. Yes White people come to Black neighborhoods to buy dope. So what? The simple, undeniable truth is that Black males are selling drugs openly, devastating Black families, and destroying Black neighborhoods with unprecedented violence. They are pretty easy to catch too. It's like shooting fish in a barrel, we often say. That is why police arrest Black males in Black neighborhoods. They go to prison (after multiple arrests), because they can't afford high-powered attorneys and more importantly, they won't stop selling illegal narcotics. (By the way, the police arrest White men in White neighborhoods, and well, you get the point.).

I didn't do a study read a report to bring you this information. I have first-hand experience on how the game goes down. The police do not as a practice, criminalize Black youth. Black youth do it to themselves because they are greedy and they want fast money. That's all there is to it. The young attorney couldn't wait to get away from me! He did not want to hear the truth. Many Black people don't want to hear it or admit it, which is why the problem has risen to the level that it has.

PROFILING 101

When police profile a serial killer, serial sniper, or serial bomber, they usually classify the suspect as a White male. Everyone (especially Black people) automatically agrees because the police know about these things, right? The accepted profile for the average shoplifter is a White female in her teens. Is that considered racial profiling? Or is it criminal profiling. So if I say that a typical drug dealer in a Black neighborhood is a Black male, is it racial profiling? Round table that for a while and get back to me.

The police always have and always will use criminal profiling to target and apprehend criminals. Criminal behavior is easy for the trained and experienced officer to predict. Even the average citizen can predict such behavior if they're paying attention. Race-based criminal profiling is similarly easy and it does happen. The police will never be able to do away with it completely, even though the very thought of it makes some groups nervous and angry.

When we were battling violent drug dealers in the eighties, we attacked on two fronts. We used criminal profiling to target Black males that sold drugs in Black neighborhoods. (For the record, White guys typically sell from inside their homes and then only to people they know). Actually it was the same tactic we used to target prostitutes. We would watch them covertly as they approached or flagged down vehicles or passing pedestrians, then made our case from there.

To get some of the customers, we used race-based criminal profiling. We watched as White people cruised the Black neighborhoods approaching or being approached by known drug dealers, which gave us probable cause for a lawful encounter. We often arrested dealer and buyer, but often let the buyer go if they willingly gave up the dealer. You see, selling crack brought a lengthier sentence than buying crack so we went after the bigger charge. Was it a racist scenario planned by the police department? No. Remember that the police don't make laws, they just enforce them. Besides, the White people still had to go to court on drug charges; it was just that the courts handled them differently. Now was that the result of intentionally racist lawmaking and judicial application? Hard to say. I do know how to beat the system. Don't engage in the illegal sales of narcotics, or hang out with people who do and you won't have to worry about it!

Racial profiling does happen but it is difficult to prove. Remember the commissioner's son, the young attorney? If he had been in a White neighborhood driving what I call a ghetto clown car, and treated accordingly, then he would have had a legitimate claim. But he wasn't, so he didn't, and he ended up looking like a fool.

Our American society gives its police broad authority to stop motorists who accept the responsibility and the privilege of driving a motor vehicle. Remember folks, it is a privilege- not a right- to lawfully operate a vehicle in this country. For instance, in Florida, an officer can stop you just to see if you have a driver license, or to check the small decal on your license plate. So be careful before you go screaming racial profiling because you take away from valid cases when you make false claims. I'll show a good example of crying wolf that clearly proves my point.

Shortly after my panel encounter with the young attorney, he and his mother ramped up their attack by passing out racial profiling complaint forms to area churches and asked them to have their members fill them out if they get stopped by the police.

The following documents are an example of an uninformed Black citizen lying to be right and being manipulated by an overzealous politician who would do or say anything to make a false claim come true. This is an actual racial profiling investigation and I am obliged to share it with you.

ATTACHMENT A

Incident Report # <u>2006-SR-0221</u>

PROFILING COMPLAINT FORM

FORWARD TO INTERNAL AFFAIRS VIA CHAIN OF COMMAND NO LATER THAN END OF TOUR OF DUTY

Completed by Supervisor:

_____Sergeant _____   8-10-06_____
     (Name/Employee #):   Date of Contact

Name of Complainant(s): <u>Ms. ▮▮▮▮▮</u>
R/S: <u>B/F</u> Address ▮▮▮▮▮<u>Orlando FL 32808</u> Telephone #407-▮▮▮▮▮

Witnesses: _____
R/S: _____Address _____Telephone #_____

Name of Officer(s): <u>Ofc. Derwin Bradley</u>
R/S: <u>B/M</u> Unit # <u>69106</u> Employee ▮▮▮▮▮

Location of Occurrence: <u>1600 block Mercy Drive</u>

Citizen Complaint:

Ms. ▮▮▮alleges that she pulled out in front of Officer Bradley's patrol vehicle on Mercy Drive and was stopped by the officer. She states the officer approached her vehicle with his gun aimed at her. She states that she feels she was threatened with lethal force because she is black.

<u>(See Citizen's Complaint attached)</u> _____ _____
Signature   Date   Notary

Officer Response (Reason for stop in detail):

Officer Bradley states that Ms. ▮▮▮ pulled out in front of his marked patrol vehicle onto Mercy Drive, causing him to have to stop abruptly to keep from crashing into her. He stated that when she stopped in a parking lot, Ms. ▮▮▮ immediately opened the driver's car door. Officer Bradley stated that it was dark (2045 hours) and he could not tell who was driving the car. He stated that he pulled his handgun out for his own safety as he approached the vehicle. He gave loud verbal commands for the driver to close the car door. Officer Bradley stated that he kept his gun muzzle pointed down and denied pointing his weapon at Ms.▮▮▮. He stated that once he saw it was an elderly female, he holstered his weapon. Officer Bradley stated that he was very concerned for his safety when he saw the driver's door opening and was trying to maintain his officer safety.

_____   ___<u>8-10-06</u>_____
Signature   Date

1 of 2

SR 2006-SR-0221/Bradley
Page 2

Officer Bradley was working in the Mercy Drive area due to recent shootings, drug activity, and weapon violations. I told her that he did not violate any department policy by having his gun in a ready position ; he approached her vehicle. He was concerned for his officer safety. I told her that I would make a note (her complaint but that I did not feel he violated any policy. She disagreed and stated she didn't feel a wh lady would have experienced the same treatment. The call ended upbeat but she did not agree with my findings. I thanked her for bringing the incident to my attention.

I have discussed this complaint with Officer Bradley and I do not see a need for any further action.

Respectfully submitted,

███████████ ██ ████████

Sergeant ███████████
North Patrol Division

Chain-of-Command	Reviewed	Date
Lieutenant	_____	_____
Captain	_____	_____
Deputy Chief	_____	_____
Internal Affairs	_____	_____

*Upon completion by Supervisor, forward this form via the employee's chain-of-command and return to the submitting Investigator from Internal Affairs Section. This form shall be attached to the original Supervisory Referral located in the Internal Affairs Section.

Internal Affairs Section
SUPERVISORY REFERRAL RESPONSE FORM

Supervisory Referral:　　　　**2006-SR-0221**

*Completed by Supervisor (Name/Emp. #):　　　　　Sgt. ████████████

Return to Internal Affairs no later than:　　　8-15-06

Name of citizen(s):　　　　Ms. ████████

Method of contact:　　　　Phone

Date and Time of contact:　　8-14-06 1300 hrs

HOW RESOLVED:

On July 13, 2006 Officer Derwin Bradley conducted a traffic stop with Ms. ████████ in the 1600 block of Mercy Drive. On August 1, 2006 Ms. ████ came to OPH to file a Profiling complaint against the officer. She stated in her written complaint that Officer Bradley engaged in racial profiling because he pulled his gun out and aimed it at her. She stated that she is 73 years old and is incapable of hurting anyone. Ms. ████ stated that a white lady under the same circumstances in a white neighborhood would have never been approached at gunpoint.

I spoke with Officer Bradley concerning the complaint. He stated that he stopped Ms. ████ vehicle in the 1600 block of Mercy Drive. He stated that it was dark (2044 hours) and he could not see inside the vehicle to see who was driving. He stated that as he approached the vehicle, Ms. ████ started to open the driver's door. Officer Bradley stated that he did draw his weapon and give verbal orders for Ms. ████ to stay in the car. He stated that he had his firearm pointed down in a ready gun position and never pointed it at Ms. ████. He stated that as soon as he saw the driver was elderly, he holstered his weapon. Officer Bradley then obtained Ms. ████ driver's license, explained the reason for the stop, returned the license, told Ms. ████ to be careful and cleared the traffic stop with a verbal warning.

I then was able to make contact with Ms. ████ by phone. She reiterated the information stated in her written complaint. She denied ever opening her driver's door and stated she was very concerned that the officer stood behind her driver's door during the stop. I explained that we are trained to stand in that position during traffic stops for our safety. I then asked Ms. ████ if her vehicle has tinted windows. She stated that her vehicle windows are tinted and she could understand how the officer would have a hard time seeing inside the vehicle to see who was driving the vehicle. I asked at what point the officer holstered his weapon. She stated he put the gun away after he approached her car.

I explained to Ms. ████ that she did everything a reasonable person would do during the traffic stop and that if she is ever pulled over again, she should do everything the same way. I explained to Ms. ████ that

Profiling Complaint Form (continued)

Investigation:

Since June 2006, Officer Bradley has been assigned to the Mercy Drive area as part of Operation Felony Focus. During his patrol duties, he almost crashed into Ms. ██ when she pulled her vehicle onto Mercy Drive in front of the patrol vehicle. Ms. ██ acknowledged that she saw Officer Bradley's vehicle but that she "pulled out too quick." However, she adamantly denied opening her car door. She stated that Officer Bradley pointed his gun at her. She feels that a white lady driving in a white neighborhood would not have been approached by gunpoint. Ms. ██ stated that she has tinted windows on her vehicle. Officer Bradley acknowledged having his handgun drawn but stated that it was pointed down in a ready gun position. He stated that he did this for officer safety reasons.

In reviewing the circumstances of the traffic stop, it is evident that Officer Bradley had a legitimate reason for stopping Ms. ██. She committed a traffic infraction and almost caused a crash. This incident occurred in an area that has a high level of arrests for drug activity, felony crimes, and weapons charges. For the past three months, Officer Bradley has been taken out of his district in College Park to provide extra patrol in this area. When Ms. ██ opened her car door quickly, Officer Bradley was justified in being concerned for his officer safety. He could not see the occupant due to the dark parking lot and tinted windows on the vehicle. He did not know the driver's intentions. When he saw the driver was elderly, Officer Bradley reholstered his weapon, asked Ms. ██ for her license, explained the reason for the stop, returned the license, told Ms. ██ to be careful and cleared the traffic stop with a verbal warning.

Resolution:

☐ Complainant satisfied with supervisor's intervention.
☐ Supervisory notes/counseling.

☐ Inconclusive. *
X No merit. *

*Explain. In handling calls with Officer Bradley in College Park, I have seen Officer Bradley draw his weapon and keep it at the ready gun position in situations that call for heightened officer safety precautions. I do not feel that Officer Bradley's actions were racially motivated. I feel he was trying to stay safe while doing his job. Ms. ██ seems to have done everything a reasonable person would do when encountering a police officer. However, due to his training and experience, Officer Bradley perceived the situation as a possible threat to his officer safety, something a civilian would not necessarily perceive. This complaint has been discussed with Officer Bradley and I do not see a need for any further action.

☐ Formal Investigation

Chain of Command	Approved/Disapproved	Date	For Internal Affairs Use Only
Lieutenant	_____	_____	
Captain	_____	_____	Complainant Notified
Deputy Chief	_____	_____	Yes ☐ No ☐
IA Manager	_____	_____	
Prof Stds Captain	_____	_____	Date _____
Chief of Police	_____	_____	

OP 61A.FORM.P&P 10/17/02

```
 8/09/2006                Orlando Police Department 7.04            PL9051F
 10:06:44                     Incident Report                      PAGE:
```

Incident Numb : 2006-00262051
Incident Type : 1050   STOPPING VEHICLE

```
                   Call        Dispatch      Arrive        Clear
 Date. . . . . :   7/13/2006   7/13/2006     7/13/2006     7/13/2006
 Time. . . . . :   20:44:35    20:44:35      20:44:35      20:47:22
 Location. . . :   1600 MERCY DR
 Cross Street. :
 Nature of Call:
 Caller. . . . :   UNKNOWN
 Complainant . :   UNKNOWN

 Grid. . . . . :   GRID#-1079      Subgrid . . . . : GRID 1079C  Distr: D-B3
 Phone . . . . :                   DOW . . . . . . : THURSDAY
 License Plate :                   License State . :
 Source. . . . :   On Patrol       Report Required : NO
 Priority. . . :   6               Operator. . . . : NORTH
 Recv. by. . . :                   Dispatch by . .
 Unit 1# : T75       ID# 1: BRADLEY,DERWIN,J,       ID# 2:
 Unit 2# :           ID# 3:                         ID# 4:
```

Original Information

```
 Location. . . : 1600 MERCY                Type. . : 1050    STOPNG VEH
 Cross Street:                             Priority: 6
```

Incident Narrative
No Narrative

Disposition

Date	Time	Disposition	Unit	ID#1	ID#2
7/13/2006	20:47:22	V	T75	BRADLEY,DERWIN,	
7/13/2006	20:47:22	BF	T75	BRADLEY,DERWIN,	

UNIT LOG

```
 Time        Unit Last Command Name #1        Additional Information
 20:44:35 T75  Creat Incd  BRADLEY,DERWIN,
 20:47:22 T75  Clear Unit  BRADLEY,DERWIN,
```

Unit Summary

Unit	Officer 1	Officer 2	Dispatch	Arrive	Clear	Minutes
T75	BRADLEY,DERWIN,		20:44:35	20:44:35	20:47:22	3

```
 Total Units:   1      Total Number of Minutes:      3
```

Orlando Police Department

Investigation Report

Case Type:	Supervisory Referral			**Case #:**	2006-SR-0221
Call Type:	Traffic Stop	**Incident Date:**	07/13/2006	**Time:**	20:45
Origin:	Citizen	**Date Reported:**	08/01/2006	**Time:**	8:00
Report #:	2006-262051				
Location:	1600 Mercy Drive				
Sector:	B	**District:** 3			
Status:	Open			**Date Closed:**	

Complainant(s)

Complainant: ▮▮▮▮▮▮

Address: ▮▮▮▮▮▮

City:	Orlando		**State:**	FL	**Zip:**	32808

Home Phone 407-▮▮▮▮▮

Notes:

Employee(s)

Employee: Bradley, Derwin J **ID:** ▮▮▮▮

Supervisor: ▮▮▮▮▮▮ **ID:** ▮▮▮▮

Notes:

Allegations

Type:	Regulations	**Title/Name:**	Misconduct
Violation:	900-7 Conduct Toward the Public		
Finding:		**Finding Date:**	
Notes:			

Assignments

Group:	Bureaus	**Assigned To:**	Patrol Services
Assign Type:	Supervisor	**Assign By:**	████████
Assign Date:	8/1/2006	**Due Date:**	8/15/2006
Completion Date:		**Recommendation:**	
Notes:			

Notifications

Exhibits

Narrative:

On 08-01-06 a citizens complaint form was received by IA in reference to a complaint on Ofc. D. Bradley. In the letter ████████ advises that she was stops on a traffic stop by Ofc. Bradley. ████ stated that she pulled out in front of the marked police car, that it was approximately 4 car lengths away from her. She pulled over into a parking lot were the officer exited his vehicle with his firearm aimed at her. Ofc. Bradley asked her for her license to which she provided. Soon there after Ofc. Bradley returned her license and told her to be careful. No citation was issued.

████ states that she is a 73 year old woman and incapable of hurting anyone. She was fearful that the firearm could have gone off and struck her. She believes she was stooped and this "intimidation" was used because she is black.

A supervisory referral form and a racial profiling form will be sent to Sgt. ████████ to be returned to IA by 08-15-06.

2

12:20P FROM:ORLANDO POLICE INTER 4072463916   TO:94072360444   P.2⁄4

CITIZEN'S COMPLAINT

Complaining Party: ████████ ████████

Address: ████████████████ Orlando Fla 32808

Telephone No.: 407 - ████████

Complaint Against: Police Department

Employee No.:

Complaint:

Date: 7-13-06

Time: 8p & 9p

Place: Mercy Drive

Nature of the complaint: Racial profiling, Unnecessary use of force + intimidation. See attached.

```
RECEIVED
JUL 3 1 2006
INTERNAL
AFFAIRS
```

In July 2003, Florida State Statute 112 was amended, giving officers the right to sue a complainant for duty-related injuries for knowingly filing a false complaint [FSS 112.532(3)].

I, ████████████████, do hereby swear (or affirm) that the factual allegation(s) made by me above in this Citizen's Complaint are true and based upon fact.

████████████████

Complaining Party

I authorize members of the Citizen Police Review board to review relevant photographic evidence regarding my case.

Yes ████████████ (Sign)   No_____ (Sign)

Subscribed and sworn to before me this 28th day of July, 2006
████████████████

Notary Public/State of Florida
At Large. My commission expires:

(Notarial Seal)

```
NOTARY PUBLIC
STATE OF FLORIDA
████████████████
MY COMMISSION # DD 517494
EXPIRES: February 13, 2010
1-800-3-NOTARY    FL Notary Discount Assoc. Co.
```

AD-28D.P&P 3/1/04   Page 1 of 3 Pages

CITIZEN'S COMPLAINT (CONTINUED)

On July 13,2006, i was traveling North on
Mercy Drive. After the passenger in my Car
Reminde me that i had ice Cream in the Car.
i turned around to head Southbound on Mercy
Drive. After turning Left into a side Road
and Reentering into Mercy Drive, i headed Back
Southbound. Uhn doing So, pulled in Front of
a police Car then was Approximately 4 Cars length
of distance Between the two Cars. the officer
immediately flashed his light to pull me over. i
pulled over into a Church parking lot. the officer
approached my vehicle with his gun aiming at
me and ordered me not to get out of the Car.
i Rolled the Window down he asked for my
License. i gave it to him. he asked whether
i saw him. i said i did see him but i guess
that i pulled out to quick. he handed me back
my License and told me to be Careful.
i am a 73 year old Woman that is incapable of

_____
Complaining Party

AD-28D.P&P 3/1/04   Page 2 of 3   Pages

CITIZEN'S COMPLAINT (CONTINUED)

hurting anyone, that gun could have gone off and killed me. this is Racial profiling because one Old white Lady Under the Same Circumstances in a white Neighborhood would have Never been approached by gun point. this is the type of Unnecessary force that Only Serves to intimidate Black. Just because I'm Black does not Mean you Can get away with such threat of Lethal force violence.

Complaining Party

AD-28D.P&P 3/1/04   Page 3 of 3 Pages

█████ POLICE DEPARTMENT
CITIZEN'S COMPLAINT

Complaining Party:_____

   Address:_____

   Telephone No.:_____

Complaint Against:_____

   Employee No.:_____

Complaint:

   Date: _____

   Time: _____

   Place: _____

   Nature of the complaint:_____

_____

_____

_____

_____

_____

_____

_____

I, _____, do hereby swear (or affirm) that the factual allegation(s) made by me above in this Citizen's Complaint are, to the best of my knowledge and belief, true and based upon fact.

_____
Complaining Party

Subscribed and sworn to before me
this _____day of _____20____

_____
Notary Public, State of Florida
At Large. My commission expires: (Notarial Seal)

████████

Page ____of____Pages

100 South Hughey Ave
Orlando, FL 32802-0913
407-246-3929
----- Forwarded by▓▓▓▓▓/OPD/Orlando on 08/15/2006 10:50 AM -----

▓▓▓▓▓▓▓▓▓▓

08/14/2006 03:00 PM

▓▓▓▓▓▓▓▓▓▓▓▓▓▓▓▓▓
▓▓▓▓▓▓▓▓▓▓▓▓▓▓▓▓▓
▓▓▓▓▓▓▓▓▓▓▓▓▓▓▓▓▓
▓▓▓▓▓▓▓▓▓▓▓▓▓▓▓▓▓
▓▓▓▓▓▓▓▓▓▓▓▓▓▓▓▓▓
▓▓▓▓▓▓▓▓▓▓▓▓▓▓▓▓▓
▓▓▓▓▓▓▓▓▓▓▓▓▓▓▓▓▓
▓▓▓▓▓▓▓▓▓▓▓▓▓▓▓▓▓
▓▓▓▓▓▓▓▓▓▓▓▓▓▓▓▓▓

cc
SubjectFwd: Badges- (LAPD) Officer Injured in Rifle Attack

----- Message from "Ronald M. Thomason" <r4445@cox.net> on Mon, 14 Aug 2006 05:15:21 -0700 -----
To:badges@1badge.com
Subject: Badges- (LAPD) Officer Injured in Rifle Attack

"Police said that after stopping the Honda, Perez charged them,
firing the AK-47, raking the patrol car with bullets that pierced its
windshield. "It's a miracle that neither officer was killed," Lt.
Paul Vernon said in a news release."

<http://www.latimes.com/news/local/la-me-officer14aug14,1,3679247.story?coll=la-headlines-california>

From the Los Angeles Times
Officer Injured in Rifle Attack
James Tuck's left hand is nearly severed when a man fires on his
police car with an AK-47.

By Stuart Silverstein
Times Staff Writer

August 14, 2006

Doctors at USC University Hospital performed emergency surgery late
Sunday to save the hand of a rookie officer with the Los Angeles
Police Department who was struck down in an assault-rifle attack,
authorities said.

The officer, James Tuck, 26, was wounded by at least three bullets
fired Saturday night from an AK-47 by a passenger who jumped from a
stolen car in the Montecito Heights area.

The shooting came after Tuck and his partner stopped a black Honda Accord that they suspected was stolen.

Authorities said one bullet nearly severed Tuck's left hand at the wrist and it was uncertain whether specialists would be able to save it.

They said that Tuck, who also was wounded in his lower back and struck in the stomach by a bullet that passed through his protective vest, was in serious but stable condition and that his life was not in jeopardy.

Police Chief William J. Bratton called the shooting "an attempted assassination of two police officers," referring to Tuck and his training officer, 18-year LAPD veteran John Porras, whose face was cut by glass fragments.

Porras was able to return fire and wounded the suspect in the leg.

Noting that both occupants of the Honda were arrested near the scene within 90 minutes of the 11 p.m. Saturday shooting, Bratton credited Tuck and Porras' "quick reactions and excellent training for keeping these two violent criminals from getting away."

Police provided limited details about Tuck. They indicated, however, that he is within a couple of months of completing his probationary period after graduating from the Police Academy nine months ago, and that he is the brother of another LAPD officer.

Police said his brother and parents were by his side at the hospital.

According to police, the suspected shooter faces charges of attempted murder of police officers.

He was identified as Jose Perez, a 31-year-old resident of Montecito Heights. He was being held at Los Angeles County Jail, with bail set at $2 million.

The name of the other suspect, who was described as a Latino male in his 30s, was not released.

Officials said they were evaluating whether to charge him with attempted murder of police officers and driving a stolen vehicle.

The shooting took place on Sierra Street, just north of Flora Avenue near Lincoln High School.

Police said that after stopping the Honda, Perez charged them, firing the AK-47, raking the patrol car with bullets that pierced its windshield. "It's a miracle that neither officer was killed," Lt. Paul Vernon said in a news release.

After Perez was shot in the leg, police said, he dropped his rifle and fled, but was quickly arrested in a nearby yard and taken to a local hospital for treatment.

The other suspect drove off but abandoned the Honda on Gillig Avenue, a block north of the shooting.

He was arrested after tips from residents led them to where he was hiding under a vehicle, police said.

Police later determined that the Honda had been reported stolen from northeastern Los Angeles on July 28.

A spokesman said the vehicle had paper dealer license plates even though it was a late-1990s model Honda.

Bratton scheduled a news conference for 10 a.m. today to discuss his concerns about the rising number of firearm assaults on police this year.

Ron Thomason
Las Vegas, NV 89146

"Courage is endurance for one moment more."

Badges mailing list
Badges@1badge.com
http://1badge.com/mailman/listinfo/badges

So what do you think? Was she racially profiled? I think you all know the answer to that question. Did you read the article on the shooting in California? That is the main reason why I do traffic stops the way I do.

Contrary to popular belief, I have no desire to lay down my life for this job. However, I am absolutely willing to risk death to help a citizen or fellow officer.

One of my military counter-terrorist instructors used to tell us, "If you must err, err on the side of violence." Of course counter-terrorism is a much different game, so let me clarify. What that means in civilian law enforcement terms is that I would rather upset you or hurt your feelings than to have the Chief hand my mother a folded flag at my funeral.

Anyone that knows me knows that I am consistently tactical. I always strive to put myself in a superior position so if things go bad, I will have the advantage. I really don't care what race you are or if you're male or female. Even age is not a factor in my book (unless a child is involved). My survival comes first and that's all there is to that. Again, if you get frightened or get your feeling s hurt, I'm willing to suffer that.

I spent the last several years working in an affluent White community in Orlando. These people are generally polite to the police and actually smile and wave when they see them. It was quite a switch from working in a Black neighborhood. But don't let those smiles fool you, I've gotten plenty of complaints sent to the Mayor's office as well as the Chief, about my tactics, which are all well within department guidelines. I've never been found at fault for my actions.

THE CASE OF THE MIFFED VICE PRESIDENT...

In 2004, during one of the major hurricanes that slammed Orlando, I responded to a silent alarm at a property with a mansion and a two-story guesthouse. I came around the back of the main house and found a grungy-looking White male in his mid forties and a teenager near the back door. I saw no vehicle in the area so I figured them for burglars trying to take advantage of the storm. I ordered them to sit on the ground and keep their hands on top of their heads. I was in a bad position, standing alone with these two between the two houses on this huge property. I asked the man if there was anyone else on the property. He said no, and then tried to explain why he was there. I told him that if anyone tried to jump me from behind, I would shoot him first, and I meant it. I held my gun at the low-ready position (45-degree angle at the ground), like I always do and waited for back up. It turned out that the man was a Senior Vice President of a major corporation and his boss owned the mansion. He was there trying to drain water out of the basement. Well, he wrote a four-page letter to the Mayor and told him that I pointed my gun at his thirteen-year-old son and also threatened to kill him. (Lying to be right!). When they called me up to Internal Affairs to interview me about it, I told them what they already knew. I told them exactly what I said and why. They of course had no choice but to dismiss the complaint because I acted well within departmental guidelines.

One of the most ignorant statements Black people make to police make is, "You wouldn't do that in a White neighborhood." I always ask, "How do you know? You don't live in a White community so what's your point of reference? As always, it was an assumption, and we all know what happens when we assume (ass-u-me), right?

MORE OF WHAT YOU DON'T KNOW....

The Charlie Sector of North Patrol Division encompasses several affluent White neighborhoods/communities. Every morning, one of my White co-workers would calibrate his Radar gun in our parking garage, and then head out to the newest and hottest upscale community in Orlando. This particular community has million-dollar homes and is home to several prominent Central Floridians and a United States Senator. Nevertheless, he sets up his operation and proceeds to write White people traffic citations. A Hispanic female officer on the same squad does the same in her predominantly White district.

I personally hate writing tickets so I don't stop vehicles any more or less than I did when I worked in the Black communities.

Listen folks, no one likes to get stopped by the police. White people don't like getting stopped any more than Blacks or Latinos or Asians. I'll share with you a little secret; the most challenging people for me to stop are White men or Black women. They are the ones that have complained on me the fastest and the loudest!

Here's a breakdown of behavioral patterns that I've seen in the different types of people that I've stopped.

White women apologize, flirt, or cry. White men apologize, complain, or try to buddy-up. Black men pout or whine. Hispanic men try to cool-talk or charm. Hispanic women apologize or clam-up. Black women complain or question. Asian women clam up. Asian men clam up. Young men with money, regardless of race, smart off or try to insult. They all will lie to get out of a ticket. They all open the door and try to get out of the vehicle. They all get a pistol pulled on them and ordered back into their vehicles. No exceptions! It's all so insane! The bottom line is that no one likes to be stopped, not even off-duty police officers!

So before you go screaming racial profiling and make a fool of yourself, make sure that it is! Look at all of the factors of the stop. Where are you? What time of day or night is it? What questions does the officer ask? Does the officer ask to search your car? Does the officer write a ticket right away or does he or she start interrogating you about things that have nothing to do with a traffic infraction? Those last two scenarios are prime indicators that you are probably being profiled. (For you known drug dealer types, it means that somebody probably dimed you out).

The best thing you can do is ask a police officer that you know personally- maybe they will tell you honestly if you've been profiled.

If you are a law-abiding citizen with nothing to hide, obviously you can let an officer search your vehicle without fear of them finding something illegal. I personally would never agree to a search of my vehicle unless the officer had sufficient probable cause, or a warrant. You can refuse a vehicle search and I suggest that you do so. An officer is required to have seen, heard, or smelled something illegal in your vehicle to search your vehicle without your permission. The officer should inform you that he is conducting a lawful investigation, or has a warrant, and that he is going to search your vehicle. At that point, do not interfere or you will get arrested. Keep calm (and quiet), and get names, business cards, vehicle numbers, or vehicle license plate numbers before they leave.

For you criminals that are conducting illegal activities, you're on your own. I hope they nail your butts! Good people, if you are coerced into a search or have your vehicle searched against your will, get the information that I instructed you to get earlier and file a formal complaint with the department's Internal Affairs investigators and consult with a competent attorney and fight back.

For the record, a typical traffic stop should only take ten or twenty minutes (to write a ticket or do a computer check). Some times the computers are slow, but the stop really shouldn't last much longer than that. Remember, the more you talk or protest, the longer you're going to be there.

YOU HAVE RIGHT TO REMAIN CALM...

In keeping with my storytelling ways, here are some stark reminders of what could happen when you lose your cool during a police encounter.

These incidents are taken from my, 'Don't let this happen to you file' so...don't let this happen to you!

-**Rodney King**: Need I say more?

-**Congresswoman Cynthia McKinney**: Struck a Capital Police Officer after he stopped her at a security checkpoint. She committed a felony by battering a Federal Law Enforcement Official, and then claimed racial profiling to attempt to cover her blunder. So, on national (and international) news, she further damaged national Black credibility by maintaining that she was racially profiled.

Even if it were true, her claim lost all validity when she struck the officer. If she had done that with a street officer on a traffic stop, she would have found herself handcuffed and hauled off to jail, and rightfully so. Even her congressional colleagues were smart and distanced themselves from the clown show.

-**Major Campbell**: This one is my personal favorite. This pathetically hilarious scenario involved a Black off-duty South Florida police Major and several Orange County Deputies. A deputy stopped the Major's vehicle on the Turnpike for some minor traffic infraction. As you watch the video, you can see the Major begin to lose his cool. He probably felt that he had been racially profiled and was going to have none of it! Or it's quite possible that felt that he was above the law and didn't have time for street cops to be stopping him. He was out of his car screaming and yelling at the deputy as if he were scolding a child. The deputy told the Major to calm down and called for back up. The Major finally decided that he was not going to play anymore and began walking to his SUV. The deputy ordered him to stop and when the Major didn't, he sprayed him with pepper spray. The back-up units arrived and they all pounced on the screaming Major. Of course he was arrested and hauled off to jail. The whole thing might have been hilarious if it weren't so pathetic. Was the good Major profiled? Hard to say, and even harder to prove now.

Rumor has it the deputy that stopped the Major is thought to be as a racist and a sexist loudmouth. Unfortunately, the Major lost his cool and began acting like a common street thug and ended up in jail. He probably ended up beating the charges, but he still went to jail and he looked like an out-of-control madman on national television.

Shortly after that colorful incident, a White deputy that I did not know approached me and gave me more information on the deputy in question. (Who had since been transferred to the Criminal Investigation Division). He told me to watch the papers because that deputy was going to be brought up on sexual harassment charges for suggesting that a female subordinate wear shorter and tighter clothing if she wanted to take time off for vacation. A week or so later, the article came out and outlined all of the deputy's dirty deeds. The deputy survived the scandal despite all of the damning evidence.

-**Unknown suspect**: Pay close attention to this one folks.

A year or so later, that same deputy got behind a car that matched the description of a vehicle being sought in a homicide case. The driver, a Black male, and the passenger, a Black female, also matched the description. The deputy thought that he had hit the jackpot. When he tried to stop the vehicle, it fled. Now everything was all but confirmed and the chase was on. I listened in on the chase as the man lead deputies through the city at speeds up to one hundred miles per hour, (at about 0930 am). One can only imagine what the young lady in the car was thinking and feeling. The chase ended when the man jumped out of the car and tried to run into a lady's house. Our favorite deputy chased him and confronted him. The deputy said that the man made a motion as if to go for a weapon so he shot and killed him. No weapon was found on or near the man. As it turned out, the man fled because he had a suspended driver license. He was not the murder suspect. Before you get angry, remember that it was the man's own irrational behavior and actions that got him killed. The deputy was cleared because he thought that he was chasing a murder suspect.

So now you see how aggressive and irrational behavior during a police encounter can cost you your freedom, your health, and in some cases, your life. Be smart, be quiet, and be cool. Document everything if you feel as though you've been wronged. Finally, you may encounter a racist or mean-spirited officer who might use race, age, or gender as a pretext for a stop, but the more likely scenario is that you just got caught driving poorly, as most Americans do. Don't get angry, I have the numbers to back up my remarks. Last year 18,600 people died in vehicle crashes. Enough said!

Racial-profiling complaints received by the Orlando Police Department in recent years:

-2002: 29

-2003: 9

-2004: 7

-2005: 6

-2006: 2

Of the 53 complaints, two were ruled 'inconclusive'. Investigators determined the rest were unfounded.

SOURCE: Orlando Police Department/*Orlando Sentinel*

SECTION V-SOCIAL ATTITUDES AND THE MEDIA

"What you see is what you get."

-ANONYMOUS

In this section the Covenant's author makes a true statement when she says that not all police are racist. I'm going to add that not all White officers are racist and not all racist officers are White. Prejudice comes in all colors- but you all know that, don't you?

The Covenant author also claims that the media has created an image of the young Black male 'super-predators.' On this I agree. However, I see these young men and boys more as super violent, ruthless, and callous criminals and that image is actually very real and is aggressively promoted by... well, young Black males seeking some measure of social power. They promote it in their music and their videos. They play it in their cars and sing along! They promote it in the way that they behave. They promote it in the way that they dress, walk, and talk. They project it with the weapons that they carry. Then they promote it by inflicting violence on their women and communities. Read on...

BOYS WILL BE BOYS....

In late 2005 I rescued a young lady from her extremely violent baby-daddy who watched the original responding officer take the report and leave, then came after the girlfriend with pistol in hand (while she held her baby). I had to stand guard with my AR15 while the battered and terrified young lady and her mother gathered her things.

I then escorted them to a safe place and searched the house before leaving. In early 2006 I received a call from the young girl's mother that she had gone back to her boyfriend and was being abused. It was then that I learned that the young man had murdered a woman in front of her child during a home invasion but beat the charges because the prosecutor refused to give the only witness immunity from prosecution. The crew that he ran with were all known shooters. I organized a team and went to the house, but the young lady refused to leave. The boyfriend hid in the house until we left and later sent word that he was going to kill me. I also learned that he owned at least four weapons, an AK-47, a shotgun, a revolver (used in the murder), and a semi-automatic. Finally, one Saturday morning I received a call that he had beaten her again and this time she wanted to prosecute. He hid out at his mommy's house (as they all do), and fled before we got there to arrest him. I did however; recover a fully loaded AK-47 from the front seat of his car. After we escorted her out of the city, I obtained a warrant for his arrest and he was eventually caught by another agency.

One night after returning from a nightclub with her friends, a young lady was driving past a gas station when shots were fired. She was struck in the head and died, leaving behind several small children. The incident happened over a year ago and still no one has come forth with any information about her killer. This particular gas station is a known hangout for young people after the clubs close and they often fire weapons for no reason without any regard for anyone's safety. The crime lab report at the end of this section is an example of how reckless and dangerous these young men can be. This is the same gas station where the young lady was murdered as she passed by. Luckily, this time no one was hurt because the shooters were kind enough to shoot into the overhang.

Don't get me wrong, we all know that men in general like to portray a macho attitude, but the Covenant author would have us believe that the image imposed on our young Black men is wrong and unfair. It is not. Those young men love that image! That is, until they get arrested and have to face a judge. Then they end up in prison and use that image to as a badge of honor when they are back on the streets, as is evident by their tattoos, dress, and behavior. A friend of mine would always ask me when we would see the gold-grilled, dread-locked, baggy-clothed young men; "What message are they trying to send?"

Now I know that you are still skeptical about my motives and haven't decided if you want to trust or accept what I'm saying to you. So don't. Instead, I challenge you to go to your local police agency and ask for a computer printout of calls for service in your neighborhood, or a neighborhood of your choosing. You will then see that the simple truth is that our young men are mean, violent, and out of control! This is no myth! The media only reports what happens in our society; they don't have to make it up! (Although we do know that they have been known to do so in international news.)

In his book, 'On Killing' Lt. Col. Dave Grossman tells us that interpersonal human aggression is the most feared event in a person's life. Talking before a large group is scary, but being violently beaten by another person is both physically and psychologically damaging. Our young men (and now young women), seem to thrive on being rude; verbally berating others, and even committing acts of violence and hurting people. It almost seems as if they can't distinguish between fantasy and reality: that is until they find themselves sitting in jail cell.

Truthfully, all guys like to think that they're tough, but many Black men believe that they're the baddest creatures on the planet. Men of other races have their moments too, but it's usually after a few drinks.

Here are just a few examples of some encounters with 'tough guys' that I've had this year:

-Hispanic male during a traffic stop. He got out of his car cursing and had his fists balled up. Result: Introduced to pavement in mid-sentence. Later asked, "Why'd you do me like that?"

-Russian guys at party. They were told that it was time to end the party but they refused to comply. Result: Introduced to trash can, then pavement. Later apologized from the back seat of a police car.

- Nineteen year-old White male at Universal Studios. Approached with hands up and screaming for me to shoot him with my Taser. Result: The young man and was introduced to the Taser, then the pavement. Later said. "I didn't think that you would shoot me." He will lose his EMT certification.

-Black male at the County Jail Central Booking Facility. Attacked me as I completed arrest paperwork. Result: Introduced to another prisoner, then the wall, then the floor. Carried to isolation cell by guards.

You'll notice that I didn't say that some Black men are tough. I said that they think that they are tough, that is until the police use force on them and they start whining for mommy! Don't be angry folks: as you read earlier, men from every ethnic group get the same treatment when they exhibit like behavior. The police truly are equal opportunity enforcers: we really don't care about your race when you choose to fight one of us!

Not quite what you expected to hear is it? Keep reading, it gets worse.

Florida Department of Law Enforcement	**Orlando Regional Operations Center**	500 W. Robinson St. Orlando, Florida 32801-1771 (800) 226-8521 www.fdle.state.fl.us

█████████
Commissioner

September 20, 2006

TO: ████████████████

ATTN: BRADLEY █████████

VICTIM(S): MOBILE, STATION
OFFENSE(S): Weapons Offenses
Orange County
05/13/2006

FDLE NUMBER: ██████████
SUBMISSION: 001
AGENCY NUMBER: ██████████

SUBPOENAS PERTAINING TO THIS CASE SHOULD REFER TO THE FDLE NUMBER.

██████████████

██████████
Crime Laboratory Analyst
Firearms Section

REFERENCE :

This report has reference to item(s) submitted to FDLE on May 17, 2006 by ██████████

EXHIBIT(S) :

Q1-1, Q1-2	Two fired 40 Smith & Wesson caliber Remington cartridge cases
Q1-A	One fired 45 Auto caliber Remington cartridge case
Q1-B	One fired 380 Auto caliber Remington cartridge case
Q1-C, Q1-E, Q1-F, Q1-G, Q1-I, Q1-J, Q1-Q, Q1-R, Q1-U, Q1-V, Q1-W & Q1-X	Two fired 9mm Luger caliber PMC cartridge cases and ten fired 9mm Luger caliber Winchester cartridge cases
Q1-D, Q1-K, Q1-L, Q1-M (1& 2), Q1-O, Q1-P, Q1-S & Q1-T	Nine fired 10 mm Auto caliber Remington cartridge cases
Q1-N	One fired copper jacketed bullet

RESULT(S) :

Q1-1, Q1-2	The cartridge cases were fired in the same unknown firearm. The Q1-1 cartridge case was compared to the NIBIN Database with negative results. Manufacturers of firearms with similar characteristics could include Glock and Smith & Wesson (Sigma).

████████████████████

Committed to
Service ξ Integrity ξ Respect ξ Quality

SECTION VI-ZERO TOLERANCE/ TASK FORCE OPERATIONS

"The only thing necessary for the triumph of evil is for good men to do nothing."

-EDMUND BURKE

Fortunately, at the time of this writing, I had just been assigned to a Zero Tolerance Task Force in a particularly violent part of the city. This was not my first Task Force Operation; I've served on many during my twenty years with the agency. Once again, while I'm sure that the Covenant's author meant well, I feel that the information that was put out is misleading and in some cases, dead wrong.

The author implies that police operations intentionally target Black youth in order to make criminals out them. She couldn't be more wrong. Read on.

A Task Force Operation, which involves Zero Tolerance policing, is usually implemented when crime in an area or segment of the city has gotten beyond the effects of normal patrol operations. In these cases, the local enforcement agency must resort to more aggressive policing efforts. Contrary to popular belief, Zero Tolerance policing is not usually the desire of the policing agency. Such operations are usually politically or citizen complaint driven.

Zero Tolerance Operations are implemented to combat a specific crime problem or in the case of my most current Task Force, all out, random violence.

Police administrators don't like Task Force Operations because they take much-needed officers from their regular duties, such as investigations, traffic enforcement, drug enforcement, school resource duties, etc.

Officers don't like them because their personal and professional schedules get all screwed up because of the odd hours that Task Force Operations requires them to work. Believe it or not, not all police officers want to go in and beat down Blacks in high-crime areas. Most of them get tired of the apathy and resentment from the people and say, "Just put a wall around it and let them kill each other!" Sound cruel? Well, you wanted the truth, so here it is!

Despite what you may have heard on the news, murder and violent crime is out of control nationwide. Those of us on the front lines don't have to read statistical data: we see firsthand the beaten, the battered, the traumatized, and the dead. Interpersonal violence is out of control and it spans all races, genders, and even socio-economic barriers. The reason you see more Task Force Operations in Black neighborhoods is because Blacks tend to prey on their own communities and that's when law-abiding citizens demand police action.

Task Force Operations are extremely effective in reducing crime in a targeted area if the community and police work together to keep the area under control. The Covenant author implies that innocent people get caught up in the police actions and that tragic outcomes are the norm. What she and other well-meaning outsiders forget is that innocent people are already in harm's way when the police arrive. They are already suffering when the police take over the area and begin to confront the true oppressors of Black citizens.

As for tragic outcomes, they do occur during these types of operations. Please try and remember that policing is serious and deadly business. You can't always theorize or talk your way out of situations. Sometimes you have to get down and dirty because that's all that a thug or violent criminal understands or will submit to. I know that you don't want to hear this, but this is not a movie or television show! Nor is this theory and lecture in an air conditioned classroom. This is real life and things don't always end the way you think they should.

The truth is that the only real tragedy occurs when the police do nothing, or as we call it, depolicing.

Depolicing occurs when patrol and specialized units avoid a specific area or police activity (such as traffic stops), because of politics, lack of administrative support, or excessive citizen complaints against police which result in overly aggressive supervisory write-ups or Internal Affairs investigations. Unfortunately, it is always the law-abiding citizen that ends up paying the price.

THE MISSION...

I'm going to give you a little insight into what a low-intensity Zero Tolerance Force Operation is and how it affected the citizens and officers involved.

One fine afternoon my division commander summoned me to his office. He sat me down and told me that he needed someone to work a Zero Tolerance Operation in large, well-known crime-plagued apartment complex in Northwest Orlando. I was very familiar with the complex as I had responded to numerous calls there, and recently worked a barricaded gunman call where a young man was holding his mother and younger sister hostage. Luckily we were able to resolve that situation without anyone getting hurt.

The huge complex was plagued with robberies, shootings, drug deals, carjackings, burglaries, domestic violence, and even murder. Regular patrol officers refused to patrol the area and only went into the complex when they had to. Even the specialized units avoided the area. It had become a no-man's land of uncontrolled violent crime.

The captain told me that he needed someone who could handle himself in such a dangerous environment and bring the violent offenders under control. I thought that I would be a part of a larger group that would address this well-known threat to our community. I was wrong. I was teamed with one other Black officer who had extensive knowledge of the area because he had been working out there but had recently been transferred to the Criminal Investigation Division. Needless to say, he was not thrilled to be going back into the combat zone.

The complex was a giant maze of some 250 units, all filled with young women and their children. The women of course, attracted the men, who in turn generated most of the crime. Across the street was a smaller apartment complex, which contributed greatly to the drug sales, robberies, and shootings. On either side of both complexes were single family homes that sent its representatives into the area to contribute to the lawlessness. In the middle of everything, was the only convenience store in the area.

We were given broad behavioral latitude but cautioned not to violate anyone's civil rights. We were told to ask for any assistance that we felt that we needed from the specialty units. The Tactical patrol team and the robbery detectives came out in their unmarked cars and helped us with catching fugitives and gunmen, but just about everybody else ignored our request for assistance.

Our overall mission was to suppress the violence and bring the offenders to justice. Our first task was to locate and arrest the main shooter in the area, a fifteen year-old terror who sold dope and shot and robbed people for fun. Many of his victims were so terrified of him and his crew; they refused to talk to the police or press charges. We were also tasked with hunting down the numerous fugitives in the area.

When we told other police officers what we were about to do, they frowned and asked, "Who did you piss off?" My friends and family were mortified and quickly organized a prayer group to give us spiritual protection.

ON SITE...

At the beginning of the Operation, my partner and I stood in front of the only store in the area so that we could meet everyone and learn their faces and let them learn ours. A young man in his thirties approached me and asked me whose side I was on. I asked him to clarify his question. He wanted to know if I was on the side of the agency or the side of 'the people.' I said that I was on the side of law and order and what was right. He didn't understand. I explained to him why we were there and what we intended to do. He got it. I was a little concerned that even now I have to explain to adult Black men the basics of law and order and that the police are not the oppressors. It was almost as if Black men think that they have the right to commit crimes with impunity! I know that sounds bad, but you have to talk to some of these guys to know what I'm talking about! Just for the record, that means that you have to go where they are. When you interview them in prison or jail, it's all just an act.

I really want you non-combatants and bystanders to wrap your brains around this one critical fact: there was no strong positive male leadership in this little community. The older men were either too drunk or high to be of any good, or they were just plain afraid of the youngsters. So there was no one around to control the violent young thugs. The mothers and grandmothers couldn't do it. The baby-mamas couldn't do it. The social workers didn't have a prayer. The politicians didn't even come down there and why should they? These people lived so far below the radar that they didn't even know when elections are held and they certainly didn't vote! The politicians know that so they don't even bother!

Here's what's real: the only people that can bring an area like that under control are the police, and that is exactly what we did.

Yes we were rough on them. We issued trespass warnings to those who didn't live there (for their own good) and arrested as many people as we could, for whatever we could. Sometimes we made deals to get bigger fish. We captured the main young hoodlum. You remember, the one that sold dope and liked to shoot people for fun? We captured armed robbers and carjackers; we captured burglars, baby-mama beaters, neck-breakers, and wanted men. We worked with the management to evict any woman who had violent children (it was always a young male) allowed drug dealers to hide in their apartments, or was involved in any criminal activity.

During our ninety-day tour of duty, there were several other task force operations throughout the city working to combat the rising murder rate and other violent crimes. They all came and went, but we stayed put. And still, we got almost no help from the other units. Some of the sergeants and officers that worked the area seemed to resent our presence and made no attempt to hide that fact.

AFTER ACTION REPORT...

We left the good people alone and made life hell for the troublemakers. We brandished pistols, shotguns, assault rifles, Tasers, and non-lethal launchers to let everyone know that we meant business and that we weren't backing down. Those of you who don't have the responsibility to curtail this level of violence may call our methods heavy-handed and in-your-face tactics. You are absolutely right! That was the point of the operation! We got in their faces, we intimidated, we threatened, and deterred, controlled, and arrested- and in the end, we restored order. Does that bother you? Tough. Welcome to the real world. It is good that we instilled some fear in those criminals. So what if they resented us. I recall a saying that is most appropriate: "Let them hate us, so long as they fear us!"

Besides, the only enemies that we made were the criminals and their supporters. Remember that we weren't the ones that were robbing, carjacking, and shooting people for fun. We didn't fire automatic weapons randomly in the complex without regard to the women and children that lounged and played outside. We weren't the ones conducting running gun battles back and forth across the street and through the complex because of drug deals gone bad.

We were the ones that got the desperate phone calls from terrified mothers screaming, "Please do something! I'm tired of these young boys shooting all of the time!" We were the ones that the older people in the surrounding neighborhoods came to when the young hoodlums hid out at a neighbor's house. The looks of terror and desperation on those citizens' faces shall always be with me.

I'll remind you all again that the police have the mission, duty, authority, and obligation to keep order in our society. Just for the record, during our operation we did not 'criminalize' anyone and we didn't violate anyone's civil rights. Actually, one of the worst offenders accused my partner of excessive force and he was immediately relieved of duty. The claim was disproved quickly and we went back to work.

Its like I said before, criminals are easy to catch because they can't or won't stop committing crimes. It was almost too easy! Everyone that we arrested had extensive criminal histories. Those young men made their choices long before we engaged them so we accept no responsibility for their previous standing in the criminal justice system.

I just shared with you a snapshot of what goes on inside a 'Zero Tolerance' or 'Occupation' operation. I spared you the raw violence and brutality that was suppressed by our efforts.

WHAT TO LOOK FOR IN POLICE TASK FORCE OPERATIONS

- Police management should ensure that some of the Task Force personnel reflect the community. That will cut down on the perception of racial bias during enforcement actions.

- Police should use experienced, well-trained, highly motivated officers. These types of officers tend to work well under stressful situations.

- Police management should ensure that the Task Force has experienced, strong, and competent leadership.

- Police management should set clear guidelines for rules of engagement for Task Force officers.

Those are just a few small tips for you to consider. I suggest that your community form a neighborhood watch and work closely with the police. That way you'll be kept in the loop when the police take such actions in and around your community.

SECTION VII-TIGHTEN UP!

"Image is everything."

-TONY ROBBINS

In this section, the Covenant author also speaks on police in schools and the price Black children are paying for their presence. Once again, I feel that you are being misled.

Schools are forced to have police on their campuses because of the out-of-control behavior by students. Violence and other 'at risk' behavior by students can no longer be managed by school faculty. For one, school boards across the country have banned any type of corporal punishment so there is nothing for the student to fear. Secondly, many parents refuse to discipline their children for fear of being charged with child abuse and possibly being arrested. So who is disciplining the children? No one! That's why it was necessary to put officers in the schools. I assure you that it was not something that the police wanted, but the politics of the situation demanded it be done. So once again, police managers had to drain resources to come up with the officers to man the schools until the city could hire more officers to fill their slots.

I agree that handcuffing or Tasing a small child is excessive, but middle school and high school students come in big packages and are in my opinion, fair game. Our school resource officers do a superb job of working with the students, faculty and parents, and they keep order in terribly overcrowded schools.

On the matter of Black children bearing the brunt of police action in schools, I digress to my earlier remarks. If you feel as though the system is biased against Black children, then perhaps you should focus your efforts on training them how to cope in such environments so that they're not such easy targets. It would be a heck of a lot easier than trying to force an entire system (or nation), to bend to your will or behavior patterns. Just like laws, school rules are in place for a reason. If your child breaks the rules and you support that negative behavior, then you both get what you deserve. Raise hell with the school when your child gets disciplined and you get a child who knows that they can break society's rules with your blessing- and soon even you will not be able to control them. But rest assured, if you cannot or will not control your children, society has measures in place that will.

40

STEREOTYPICAL...

Every civilized culture in the world has its stereotypes both negative and positive. The American mainstream have always frowned on any type of perceived counterculture. In the fifties it was leather jackets and slicked back hair. In the sixties and seventies it was the hippies and rock-n-roll types. Now it is the hip-hop types with their baggy clothing. Welcome to America. It is now your turn in the hot seat.

Let me ask you a question. If you were walking down the street or through a mall and you saw a group of heavily tattooed young White males wearing black shirts, blue jeans and combat boots and their heads were shaved, what would you think? Are they White supremacists, or just a group of guys who like to dress alike? What would you do?

So now your kid wants to be like everyone else and wear the latest fashions, and it just so happens that you can afford to purchase these items. So now you think that your child should be able to dress like a thug just so long as he or she doesn't act like one and the public should know the difference, right? Wrong!

People are going to think what they're going to think and there is little that you can do about it. If your child is harassed or trespassed by mall security because of dress or behavior, that's life. Malls are private property and the owners have the right to deny them entry! When you dress a certain way and project a certain image, you should expect that people might see and treat you as such. That's just human behavior. Everyone does it, even you! It's all about choice, isn't it? If you choose to dress, talk, or behave a certain way, don't expect everyone to just accept you as you are! If it were that simple there would be harmony worldwide and none of this would be relevant or necessary.

I know, I know- it's not fair! As a friend of mine always says, "The fair comes to town once a year. That's all the fair you're going to see in your life!"

Tell your children the truth about real life! Let them know that their fashion choices often determine how society treats them. Or you could just let them find out the hard way, like most parents do. It's your choice.

SECTION VIII-THE IMPOSSIBLE CHOICE

"It is the mind that maketh good of ill, that maketh wretch or happy, rich or poor."

-EDMUND SPENCER

The Covenant author writes here that Black communities are presented the impossible choice: chose safe neighborhoods and give up your civil rights. She also states that because of persistent unavailability of alternative, preventative responses to crime, equal and adequate education, job creation, and economic development, the Black community is resigned to asked for or accept more police presence and aggressive policing. These statements are so dangerously misleading that it is frightening! Let's get real for a moment! There are, and always have been alternatives to crime. It's called: *not committing crime*! Education is here for the taking! Apparently it was good enough for those who came before us and they had a lot more racism and less equipment to work with! As for jobs and other economic development, this is not some third world country where there is no industry or no jobs anywhere to be found! When I worked gangs, we regularly found jobs for anyone that wanted to work. Businesses worked with us and took good care of the young men that we sent to them. What those of us who are in touch with modern society see is a generation of young people who have no home training, discipline, basic education, or intestinal fortitude. They can't or won't keep a job or simply refuse to work for minimum wage! They can't take orders and quit as soon as the going gets tough! So they take what they think is the easy way out and engage in illegal activities.

Furthermore, if there are no economic opportunities in your area, do what immigrants have been doing since the beginning of time, move! Go to where the work is! How's that for a solution?

Anyway, it's been my experience that safe neighborhoods have little to do with the police. It's all about neighbors working together to control their surroundings. For example, if you tolerate open-air drug sales in your neighborhood, then you're going to get all of the traffic, noise, crime, and violent behavior that come with it, including increased police presence.

People who live in 'safe' neighborhoods know this and will report suspicious activity or each other at the drop of a hat. There's a reason you don't see open air drug sales in 'safe' neighborhoods or groups of young people hanging out doing nothing: their parents keep them busy! Raise and control your children so that when they become adults they learn not to crap where they eat! That's why we have bars, clubs, and other forms of entertainment! Sound like a plan? Look, the old way of thinking like a perpetual victim doesn't work. It's annoying and it makes us all look bad! You want a new relationship with Law Enforcement? Then it's time to get with the program! Maybe it's time Black communities and their leaders (if they have any), stop living in the past and look at who is really victimizing Blacks in their communities! I can assure you, that if you want to run the numbers, we'll find that no one commits more crime against Black people than Black men do! I know you didn't want me to say it but it's true, and you all know it!

The saying, "As a man thinketh, so is he", rings so terribly true here. If you think of yourselves as second-class citizens or outsiders, then that's exactly how you will behave, and that is how you will be treated. If you show resentment, distrust, and apathy toward police in your community, that is what you're going to foster in return. Most police officers really want to help you solve your problem. Help them help you.

SECTION IX-COMMUNTIY-ORIENTED POLICING

"Be firm yet not hard: soft yet not yielding"

-BRUCE LEE

My personal philosophy is that there is no such thing as Community-Oriented Policing as it pertains to agency-wide operations. Police agencies of course do have to adapt to certain cultural differences when they can, so long as it does not interfere with its primary mission- law enforcement. Many academians, sociologists, and police administrators will disagree with me because Community-Oriented Policing sounds so warm and fuzzy. The truth of the matter is that you can put some savvy officers in a certain area and get phenomenal results, but at the end of the day, a police agency must enforce the law. So in the theater of my mind, you either have a professional law enforcement agency, or you don't.

When the chief came out of retirement to run our agency, he wanted to set a new tone for us. During his first week back, he got into my car and we went for a ride. A lady ran the red light in front of me so I pulled her over. The chief ordered me not to write her a ticket, so I let her off with a warning. (The driver was a Black female on her way to work at a doctor's office.) When I got back into the car he told me that it was better to be kind than to be right. I replied, "Maybe so, but someone has to enforce the law." We continued the discussion over breakfast and as much as he tried to convince me that kinder and gentler was better, I stood my ground that we needed to maintain a professional but aggressive posture if we are to keep crime under control. I also reminded him that the bad guys probably would not subscribe to his 'kind versus right' theory. He stood his ground. Of course, being the chief, he sets the tone for the agency so I knew that he would have his way. I also knew the crime pendulum would soon swing in the opposite direction the second we began to let up and tried to play warm and fuzzy with the public.

Here's the rub, folks. As I said before, in this game you're either a professional law enforcement agency or not. There is a reason police departments have community relations units. They are the officers that provide a touchy-feely bridge between the agency and the public. As for rest of the officers, they should be focusing on professionally enforcing laws and investigating crime. Anything less and you'll see the need for Task Force Operations come upon you like the plague.

WHAT WORKS NOW

In this section the Covenant author speaks of turning around a non-supportive police department. First of all, there is no such thing as a non-supportive police department because the majority of officers are not out to get you. There are however, poorly led and poorly managed police departments that have rogue officers running amuck in the city. Only the upper management or local government leaders can force an agency to change or adapt to a community. The Black community, however, can gently persuade an agency to work closer with them by giving that which they most want to receive from the agency, <u>respect</u>.

Neighborhood Patrol Unit. This is probably the best law enforcement program that I've seen in the last twenty years. In the late eighties Orlando saw gang problem beginning to fester in its government housing complexes and other neighborhoods throughout the city. After numerous gang clashes, shootouts, and several murders, the Orlando Police Department formed its Neighborhood Patrol Units. Police managers felt that the agency had lost touch with these communities and they needed to address them with a different type of law enforcement strategy. The concept was absolutely brilliant. The agency hand picked five teams of experienced and savvy officers, one White, One Black per team, and put them into the housing projects. Offices were set up in one of the apartments in the projects. I know that some cities have housing police, but this was different. We were actually doing gang enforcement and investigations while we were building rapport with previously neglected Black citizens. The program was a huge success. Our unorthodox methods did however; cause other officers to frown on us. They thought that we were crazy to accept such an assignment. We found jobs for anyone who wanted to work. Known gang members would get kicked out of school just for being near a fight, so we would go and convince the principal to let them return. We helped a lot of gang members and their families. We put a lot of people in jail. We had lots of shoot-outs, gang fights, and even a few more deaths. The end result was that gangs were eventually suppressed and dismantled, and those officers involved became legends that are still respected in those communities. That my friends is what works. It takes a special officer to do that job; it is not for the average officer on the street. The officer must be well rounded, community-minded, and willing to think outside of the box. Most importantly though, the officers and the mission must be supported by police management, or it will not work. Let's move on!

COMMUNITY POLICING

The Covenant author writes that out of 13,500 state and local law enforcement agencies, there are only 72 citizen oversight boards. She makes it seem as though the community monitors only 0.5% of police agencies!

This is another untrue and inflammatory statement that is indicative of those who are still trying to keep you angry and uninformed. Police activity has always been and always will be watched and monitored by the media in all of its forms. Not to mention that most police departments do a better job of disciplining their employees that most businesses in this country!

Many police agencies have had cameras in their vehicles for well over a decade now. (Ever heard of the television show, *Wildest Police Chases* and similar shows?). In this country, police departments all answer to a higher municipal, county, or state authority.

A TALE OF THE TAPE...

During our Zero Tolerance Operation which I mentioned earlier, another police unit came into our area and attempted to arrest a couple of drug dealers. The dealer ran, broke into an apartment and scared the hell out of a woman and her kids. He then resisted arrest and the officers used force on him. A young man (another dealer) decided to incite the crowd and urged them to attack the officers. A small riot broke out and a brick thrown from the crowd damaged a police car. The instigator was arrested along with the other suspect.

The next day when my partner and I got to work, we questioned the residents about what happened. They told us that one of the White officers called them 'monkeys' and that it was all caught on video. I found it hard to believe that any officer would be that stupid and say or do something to mess up our operation, but I promised that I would make sure an investigation was done. All I needed was someone who was there to make a formal complaint and turn the video in. A news reporter came out and gave them her business card and told them that if she acquired the video, she would play it on television. No one came forth and I never received the video. The reporter never got a call from anyone or received a video of the incident.

So there is an example of media oversight of police. The citizens had the option of trusting the police to do an investigation or giving the evidence to the media, who would have been more than happy to air it. So unless you live in somewhere like Darfur, Sudan, you do have options for police oversight.

WAYS TO GET INVOLVED WITH YOUR LAW ENFORCEMENT AGENCY...

- -Citizen's Police Academy- Class is usually held one night a week for thirteen weeks.

- Explorer Program- School aged children learn about police work.

- -Volunteer Program- Volunteer at your local police department.

- -Citizen Observer Program- Assist your fellow citizens by patrolling your community. Contact your law enforcement agency's Community Relations Section for more information on these programs.

SECTION X-POLICE USE OF FORCE

"My actions are a result of your actions"

-BRUCE LEE

Brutality is the second most commonly and falsely or incorrectly claimed charge that citizens make against police officers, right after conduct toward the public complaints.

The Covenant author wrote that out of 4,318 incidents of POLICE VIOLENCE AGAINST AFRICAN AMERICANS (note the intentionally negative and inflammatory tone); White officers committed 3,622, or 84%. Now if you're looking for the negative, this disturbing statement is going to piss you off. The author fails to mention in this section (although it is covered negatively in another section), that White people make up the majority of police officers. Imagine that! What's the world coming to when you have mostly White officers in a mostly White country? So that being the case, it stands to reason that most Americans will encounter a White officer in their dealings with law enforcement. So would you agree that when it comes to police use of force, even White people and other ethnic groups should expect their officer to be White?

Again, if you are uninformed or just looking for a reason to be angry at the police, those vague and misleading statistics are just what the doctor ordered. You see, the numbers that were quoted only state reported accusations, they do not say if they officer was found guilty or not. Putting out this type of misinformation invokes a negative emotional response from Blacks, which I guess is the whole point.

Good news for you people who are actually looking for real solutions to real problems. I am going to show you exactly what police use of force is and how it is and should be applied. I promise you that after this section you will have a clear understanding of what police do and why they do it! And as success coach Anthony Robbins always says, "Clarity is Power!"

Most Americans, including White people, are unaware of the scope of authority that the police have. This truth applies especially to the under 30 crowd because they are not accustomed to being corrected, chastised, or physically disciplined. Unfortunately for them, when they test the police, they get a painfully rude awakening.

Several years ago, during an annual Halloween event at an Orlando theme park, I had to physically strike, detain, and arrest female subjects in four separate incidents. All were combative, all were drunk, and all were White. None of them believed that I had the authority or right to tell them what to do. They were wrong, as civilians usually are.

Remember my task force operation? At the beginning of it, we rounded up several rather unpleasant young men who began spewing obscenities and making threats, thinking that they were dealing with regular street officers. I've been teaching and training people for over twenty years so I love it when I can give someone a good lesson. I informed the young men in explicit detail of the things that I would do to them if they attempted to injure either of us. They looked at me in shock. One of them said, "You can't do that! You can't talk to me like that!" I assured him that not only could I, but I would without a second thought.

For all of the violence and havoc that these young men reaped on their community, they didn't want to be challenged or corrected by a superior force! We were the one group of people that they could not intimidate and they did not like it one little bit! Now are you starting to get the picture? Good! Let's move forward.

As I said earlier, the police are given broad enforcement powers by lawmakers and society in general. Ours is a nation of rules and laws and it is generally understood that when you break those laws, the enforcers will come and get you. Resist them at your own peril!

The police have the authority to stop, search, detain and question you if they are conducting a lawful investigation. The police can arrest you if they have a reason to believe that you have committed or are about to commit an illegal act. If you resist, they have the authority to take you down, kick you, punch you, spray you with pepper spray, shoot you with a Taser, hit you with a metal stick called an ASP Baton, or shoot and kill you if necessary. Don't like the sounds of that? Welcome to the violent world of law enforcement.

PERCEPTION IS REALITY...

In this scenario, I encountered a guy that was a lot bigger and probably stronger than I in a small room of an abandoned drug house. He took a swing at me, and I stunned him with a roundhouse kick to the head and he was arrested. I was aiming for his stomach (softer target), but he tried to duck and went face-first into my instep. The Internal Affairs sergeant that was in the room at the time thought that I used excessive force and wrote me up. Fortunately, the training sergeant approved the use of force because I used an approved technique and followed the force continuum. I gave a verbal command for him to surrender, he took a swing at me, and I knocked him out. End of story.
The sergeant who wrote me up was furious. He told me, "Well, it just looks bad when you kick people!"

I was once called in by Internal Affairs to give expert testimony when an officer and fellow martial artist was accused by another officer of improperly choking a suspect. The accusing officer thought that the other officer had used an illegal choke-hold on an arrestee. I had the accused officer show me the technique in question. I was very familiar with the Aikido move known as 'IRIMI NAGE' or 'entering throw' which involves swinging the arm across the upper torso, then bringing the person down or to a restraining hold. I assured the Internal Affairs investigators that the technique was safe and within department us of force guidelines. The officer was cleared of any wrongdoing based on my testimony.

I said all of that to say that when the police use force on citizens it always looks bad, even to other police officers and even when it really is proper and justified.

Americans have this image of 'Officer Friendly' riding down the street protecting and serving, and wearing those stupid bus driver caps, and smiling and waving at kids. Wrong answer! Americans love to hang on to stereotypes that are no longer valid! Police actually have to confront and arrest violent offenders upon occasion. You know, those sociopaths that rob, rape, steal, beat, and kill innocent victims. You remember them don't you? Did you think that they go out and commit crimes and in a moment of remorse turn themselves in? No! To put a criminal in jail, the police have to take the report, build a case, hunt them down, chase them, fight them, survive the confrontation, and transport them to jail. On top of all of that, police officers have to remain professional.

FYI: Most police agencies require that their officers experience pepper spray and the Taser before being allowed carry them on duty. I can assure you that they are both very painful experiences!

At the end of this section, I have included a copy of a police use of force matrix (we call it the Force Continuum), so that you all can get a clearer understanding of how and when we apply certain levels of force. However, you must understand one critical thing: once the police are on the scene conducting lawful duties, they are in absolute control. Challenge that authority and you will find yourself in handcuffs. Resist and you will be subdued, by whatever level of force an officer (or officers) deems necessary, even up lethal force. When an officer can't subdue a violent offender, he will call other like-minded professionals who will convince said offender to cooperate. One of the most common problems I see in Black communities is that the young men don't seem to understand how serious our business is. I can't tell you how many times that I've been told; "take that gun and badge off and I'll kick your butt!" I just laugh at them and shake my head. They act as if this is a game, so I have to remind them that their physical well-being is now in jeopardy and to submit or our next stop will be the hospital. Sometimes they get the point right away.   Sometimes they get it after I'm picking them up off of the ground, dusting them off, and asking, "Do you need medical attention sir?"

I will tell you that the police get paid to win all of the time! Fighting fair is for organized sporting events. In our job, if you lose the fight, you could lose your life!

Black people I can't stress enough the fact that you must submit to police authority just like everyone else, or pay the price, just like everyone else. I know for a fact that most police officers don't really care what race or gender you are. Resist and you will get thumped. So don't think that for a second that the laws or rules are going to change for you just because you're a minority.

I don't want to hear about past police abuses of yesteryear that the majority of you have only read about. They have no validity here! Just as you all like to say that once a person comes out prison, he or she has paid their debt to society and we shouldn't hold that past against them, give your local law enforcement agency the same benefit of the doubt.

I know that I just pissed a lot of you off and that's okay. If you read the Covenant then you probably got pissed when you read the intentionally vague brutality statistics. Well, all I can say is that I gave you all the straight-up truth. What you do with it is your own business.

What The Community And Each Individual Can Do

- -Stop acting as if the police are the oppressors of Blacks and Black communities. It is more likely that you will be beaten, robbed, carjacked, or shot by a Black male from your own community than brutalized by the police. (Run the numbers, you know I'm right).

- -Do act as if you are entitled to professional police service. Be nice to the officers and they'll be nice to you. Treat them with malice or indifference and they'll treat you the same way, or simply avoid patrolling your neighborhood and let the criminals take over.

- -The most successful, low-crime communities have Neighborhood Watch programs and meet regularly. I spent five years as a community relations officer and the biggest problem we had in some Black communities was getting the citizens to attend the meetings.

- -Teach your children to be respectful and to give simple and clear answers. Realistically, they should be more afraid of you finding out that they even had to talk to the police, than of what the officer might do. Yes sir/ma'am and no sir/ma'am go a long way with most officers. If you are in contact with the police set good examples for your children, even if the officer is clearly being unprofessional.

FYI An interview with convicted murderers of police officers gave some interesting information:

- -85% of all officers killed in the line of duty used ineffective or inappropriate levels of force.

- -The convicts also said that the officers killed were either too nice or oblivious to the threat.

If you are still confused about police use of force, I suggest you view a training video by comedian Chris Rock. It is a great tutorial for what to do during police encounters.

ATTACHMENT "A"
RESISTANCE AND RESPONSE CONTINUUM

SUSPECT'S RESISTANCE	EMPLOYEE'S RESPONSE
LEVEL I – INDICATORS OF RESISTANCE Non-verbal cues indicating subject's demeanor and attitude coupled with an apparent readiness to resist.	**EMPLOYEE'S PRESENCE** The employee's attitude and demeanor and their lawful right to be where they are.
LEVEL II – VERBAL RESISTANCE The subject's verbal responses indicating non-compliance and unwillingness to cooperate	**VERBAL DIRECTIONS** The employee's verbal communications that specifically direct the actions of the subject and offer the opportunity for compliance.
LEVEL III – PASSIVE RESISTANCE The subject fails to obey verbal direction preventing the member from taking lawful action.	**SOFT CONTROL** The employee applies techniques that have a minimal potential for injury to the subject, if the subject resists the technique.
LEVEL IV – ACTIVE RESISTANCE The subject's actions are intended to facilitate an escape or prevent an arrest. The action is <u>not</u> likely to cause injury.	**HARD CONTROL** The member applies techniques that could result in greater injury to the subject, if the subject resists their application by the member.
LEVEL V – AGGRESSIVE RESISTANCE The subject has battered, or is about to batter a person/member and the subject's action is likely to cause injury.	**INTENSIFIED TECHNIQUES** Those techniques necessary to overcome the actions of the subject, short of deadly force. If the subject resists or continues to resist these techniques there is a strong probability of injury being incurred by the subject.
LEVEL VI – DEADLY FORCE RESISTANCE The subject's actions are likely to cause death or great bodily harm to the member or another person	**DEADLY FORCE** Member's actions may result in death or great bodily harm to the subject.

ATTACHMENT "A" (Continued)
RESISTANCE AND RESPONSE CONTINUUM (TECHNIQUE GUIDELINES)

EMPLOYEE'S PRESENCE	◆ Lawful presence ◆ Attitude and demeanor ◆ Identification of authority
VERBAL DIRECTIONS	◆ Commands to direct subject action ◆ Notification of arrest ◆ Opportunity to comply

SOFT CONTROL TECHNIQUES	◆ Techniques having minimal potential of injury if resisted by a subject
	  o Pressure points
	  o Wrist locks
	  o Arm bars
	  o Compression techniques
	  o Chemical agents

HARD CONTROL TECHNIQUES	◆ Techniques having a greater potential of injury if resisted by a subject
	  o Forearm/knee/open and closed hand strikes
	  o Strikes with the baton
	  o Kicks
	  o Takedowns
	  o Head locks
	  o Impact weapons
	  o Tire deflation devices
	  o Electronic control devices (TASER)
	*Hard control techniques shall not target shaded areas indicated in Attachment B.

INTENSIFIED TECHNIQUES	◆ Techniques necessary to overcome actions of a subject short of deadly force. *Intensified techniques may target shaded areas indicated in Attachment B
DEADLY FORCE	◆ Techniques that may result in death or great bodily harm to the subject ◆ The application of deadly force is not limited to the use of a firearm, and may include application of other techniques and/or weapons.
EMPLOYEE/SUBJECT FACTORS AND SPECIAL CIRCUMSTANCES	

EMPLOYEE/SUBJECT FACTORS TO BE CONSIDERED:	**SPECIAL CIRCUMSTANCES:**
• Age • Sex • Size • Skill level • Multiple subjects or employees	• Mental incapacity • Close proximity to firearm or weapon • Special knowledge • Injury or exhaustion (member/suspect) • Disability • Imminent danger • Availability of weapons • Arrestee's level of agitation • Alcohol/drug influence • Arrestee handcuffed

ATTACHMENT B

ANATOMICAL ILLUSTRATION
(FOR USE OF HARD CONTROL TECHNIQUES, INTENSIFIED TECHNIQUES, AND DEADLY FORCE)

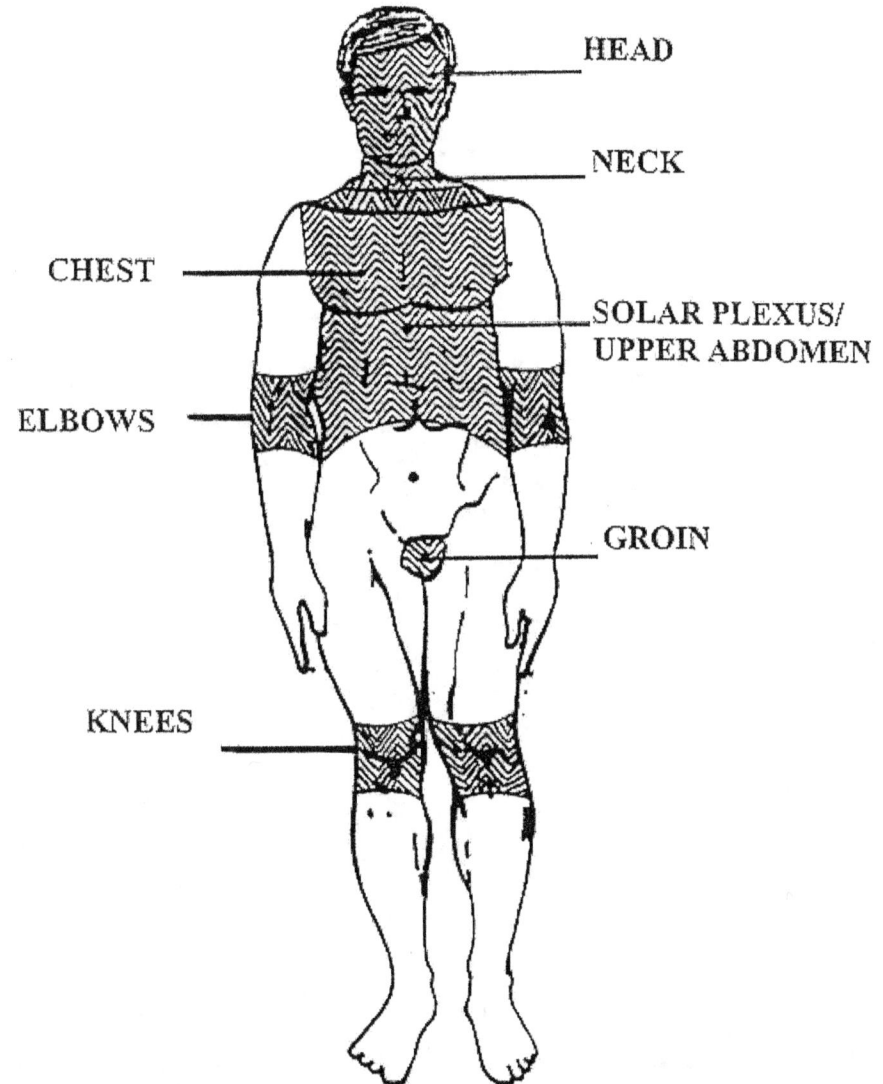

Avoid indicated shaded areas unless intensified techniques or deadly force is warranted.

Hard control techniques shall not be targeted above the shoulders, to the spine, or the solar plexus.

For TASERS, the shaded areas are approved for probe targeting. A person's head, neck, or groin areas shall not be targeted with probes. TASER Stun techniques (contact/pressure) are approved in all areas except the head and groin areas when hard control is warranted. TASER Drive Stun techniques in shaded areas below the head are approved when intensified techniques are warranted.

Targeting the head or neck with the baton or SAGE SL6 projectiles is acceptable in deadly force situations only.

ATTACHMENT B (continued)

ANATOMICAL ILLUSTRATION
(FOR USE OF HARD CONTROL TECHNIQUES, INTENSIFIED TECHNIQUES, AND DEADLY FORCE)

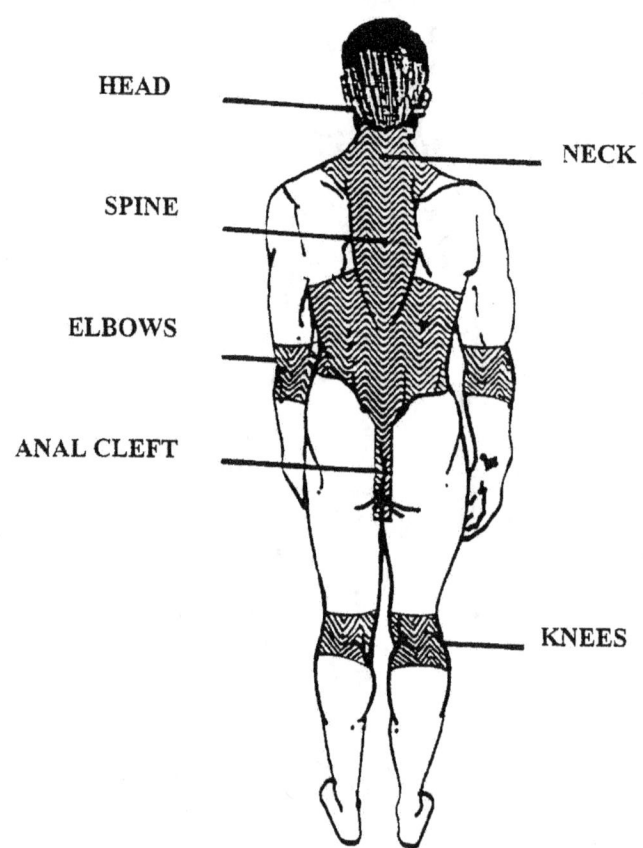

HEAD — NECK — SPINE — ELBOWS — ANAL CLEFT — KNEES

Avoid indicated shaded areas unless intensified techniques or deadly force is warranted.

Hard control techniques shall not be targeted above the shoulders, to the spine, or the solar plexus.

For TASERS, the shaded areas are approved for probe targeting. A person's head, neck, or groin areas shall not be targeted with probes. TASER Stun techniques (contact / pressure) are approved in all areas except the head and groin areas when hard control is warranted. TASER Drive Stun techniques in shaded areas below the head are approved when intensified techniques are warranted.

Targeting the head or neck with the baton or SAGE SL6 projectiles is acceptable in deadly force situations only.

P&P 1128.6 07/26/06

SECTION XI- POLICE ENCOUNTERS 101

Consensual Encounter

A police officer asks to speak to you or approaches you and begins questioning you about your actions. During this type of encounter, the officer has expressed no lawful reason to detain you. If you do not want to talk to them simply ask, "Officer am I being detained?" Or ask, "Officer am I free to leave?"

If the officer tells you that you are not being detained and are free to leave, then you have the option of walking away.

Non-Consensual Encounter

A police officer approaches you and stops or detains you. They will inform you that they are conducting a lawful investigation into some type of criminal activity. At this point you are not free to leave. You are being lawfully detained and if you make trouble, you will be arrested. This is the scenario where a lot of people get sprayed, Tased, or even shot, because they unnecessarily escalate the situation by mistakenly challenging police authority.

Traffic Stops

Traffic stops are extremely dangerous encounters for police so conduct yourself accordingly.

Stop as soon as possible when you see the police lights.

Stay in your vehicle.

Roll down your window.

Keep your hands in plain sight. Do not reach for anything unless the officer tells you to.

Keep your well-meaning passengers calm and quiet. (You know what I mean).

Surrender your license and registration upon demand. It is the law and failure to do so will result in your arrest. The officer does not have to tell you why you're being stopped before you give them your license.

Calling your attorney will not help you. The police have attorneys too- lots of them.

Interfering or Disorderly Conduct

Any action or activity that keeps the police from properly conducting their investigation can be considered interfering and you will be arrested. Those activities include but are not limited to talking, yelling, screaming, excessive movement, and physical obstruction. Drawing a crowd with loud or unruly behavior is considered disorderly conduct and you will be arrested.

Battery LEO

Malicious touching, pushing or striking a Law Enforcement Official is a felony. This act of aggression will get you thrown down, punched, kicked, sprayed, Tased, hit with a metal stick, and in some cases, shot.

Quotas

Most people think that police have to write a certain amount of tickets or make a set amount of arrests to meet a quota or get some type of bonus. Quotas are illegal for obvious reasons, as are bonuses for arrests. We are not bounty hunters. We don't get paid anything extra for catching criminals.

DIG DEEPER....

This quick message is for attorneys, friends, and families of people whose encounters with the police end tragically. The local NAACP office is next door to the police department so I often see the people who work there. I assisted one of the workers on a case where a young man died during a struggle with police officers from a neighboring city. I listened to the case and spoke with the young man's mother, who was an attorney who lived in a northeastern state. The case sounded suspicious: a Black male that led police on a short chase, then died during a fight with officers. The young man also just happened to be dating the sister of a White officer who was employed by the police department. Cocaine was found in the young man's vehicle. His mother believed that it was a set-up, and it sure looked that way. That was, until further investigation revealed that the young man had multiple arrests for possession of cocaine. His mother had no idea that he had ever been arrested or used drugs! My heart went out to her. Did the police plant drugs and commit murder? Highly unlikely, and given his history, it would be almost impossible to prove. I do know that cocaine users can die during intense physical exertion because I had a man die during a struggle with several officers and myself. He was high on crack cocaine and was on a crime spree. We wrestled with him and handcuffed him. No one ever hit him. I knew the symptoms of cocaine psychosis so I called for paramedics immediately. We turned him on his side so that he could breath. The man died before the ambulance arrived mere minutes later. Fortunately, we had plenty of witnesses (including some of his victims), and were cleared after being briefly relieved of duty.

There are a lot of variables going on during a dynamic police encounter that the average citizen just can't comprehend. When faced with such factors, always dig deeper before going public with your accusations.

YOUR CONSTITUTIONAL RIGHTS

A curse on the movie and television industry for creating what is possibly the greatest myth of all times (right after the cop and donut thing). May the fleas of a thousand camels infest your armpits!

Seriously, in virtually every movie or television show where a police officer makes an arrest, he or she begins spouting the Hollywood version of the Miranda Warnings, or the Constitutional Rights to the bad guy.

Once again, the directors couldn't be more wrong in their depiction of police operations.

Now pay attention! The police do not have to read you your Constitutional Rights unless they are going to ask you specific questions about a crime in which you are a suspect.

In other words, the police will only read you your rights if there is any chance that you might incriminate yourself or implicate yourself in a crime that they are investigating.

For example: if you are arrested for a crime such as battery, theft, or domestic violence, and a witness has written a statement against you, the arresting officer will probably not question you about that crime.

However, if you are arrested for a serious crime such as robbery, rape, arson, or murder, then it is highly likely that you will be taken to police headquarters where you will be read your rights before being questioned. In this case a detective will probably want to talk to you and he or she will read your rights to you before questioning.

For the third and final time, this ain't no movie, and it ain't no T.V. show! This real life! Artistic license is cute in Hollywood, but it does not work in the real world!

CONSTITUTIONAL RIGHTS WARNINGS

- YOU HAVE THE RIGHT TO REMAIN SILENT. DO YOU UNDERSTAND?

- ANYTHING YOU SAY MAY BE USED AGAINST YOU IN COURT. DO YOU UNDERSTAND?

- YOU HAVE THE RIGHT TO TALK TO A LAWYER BEFORE AND DURING QUESTIONING.
  DO YOU UNDERSTAND?

- IF YOU CANNOT AFFORD A LAWYER AND WANT ONE, ONE WILL BE PROVIDED FOR YOU BEFORE QUESTIONING WITHOUT CHARGE. DO YOU UNDERSTAND?

- HAS ANYONE THREATENED YOU OR PROMISED YOU ANYTHING TO GET YOU TO TALK TO ME?

- CAN WE TALK ABOUT WHAT HAPPENED?

Those are your rights. You can waive your rights and talk, or you can invoke your rights and keep quiet. It's your choice.

ON ATTORNEYS...

Contrary to Hol-lie-wood police shows, attorneys cannot storm into a police station and demand to speak to a prisoner, or stop an interrogation/interview.

Attorneys, especially privately retained ones, have no authority over the police and cannot demand that a prisoner be released. Most modern police stations are secure buildings therefore an attorney would need police permission and escort to enter.

However, if they somehow gain entry and attempted to interfere in a police investigation, they could be escorted from the building or arrested.

ON JUVENILES....

The police can detain and interview juveniles without parental consent if they are suspected of being involved in a crime. Parents cannot interfere with police investigations and cannot stop an interview. Police will attempt to make contact with the parents as a courtesy and it is usually required by departmental policy or state law.

SECTION XII-...AND JUSTICE FOR ALL?

"We have underestimated the resourcefulness of the wicked."

-ANONYMOUS

I'm not going to go into to great detail about what The Covenant covers about our justice system because I am going to cover it in a future book. Again, it quotes basically the same type of statistical data that has been put out for years. Apparently, no one is going out into the real world anymore.

A while back, I downloaded about twenty pages of letters from Florida inmates complaining about sexual abuse to Amnesty International. Prison rape is apparently off the scale, and according to the inmates, no one seems to care! Whenever I came across a young man who thought that he was ready for the thug life, I let him read some of the pages. They usually refuse to believe the letters from the inmates. I guess if I was a rapper or a thug, they would listen. But, since thugs and rappers don't like to talk about such things, our young men will continue to learn the hard way.

As I said before, a lot of those young men (and women) are in prison for a reason. Do not be fooled by sob stories! Those people made a choice, and they often make the same choice over and over again! Read on.

DECISIONS, DECISIONS...

During our Zero Tolerance Operation a Chrysler 300 was seen driving erratically down the main road. I found the car parked in the driveway of a house. I was only going to tell the driver to settle down. As I approached the car, a man that I knew came out of the house and started talking to me. I looked into the car and saw that the driver was gone and noticed that there was a passenger inside. He saw me and tried to hide a baggie of crack cocaine next to the driver's seat. He had money spread out in his lap, too. I told him not to move. He began reaching for something near his left leg. I pulled my gun and ordered him to put his hands up. My partners came and snatched him out of the car. I found a loaded 10mm pistol with an extended magazine tucked between the seat and center console that had been covered by his left leg.

I tell you this story because the young man was a convicted felon who was recently out of prison. A check via our computer revealed that the gun was stolen. I seized the drugs and the money. The driver had abandoned him, having run out of the back door of the house long before I arrived. His wife arrived shortly afterwards. He was supposed to be cashing his check (yes, he had a job), paying rent, and getting his butt home so that he could spend time with his children. My heart went out to his wife because possession of firearm by a convicted felon could mean twenty years in prison! My young friend had made another bad decision, and it is going to cost him dearly. What's really sad is that his story is so common among Black men, it is frightening.

I have a question: If the system is so bad, why do these men keep going back? Apparently prison rape is either overstated, or it is not as unpleasant to them as we thought. Something to think about ladies.

Another question: If you believe that the American justice system is unequal to Blacks, why won't you stop committing crimes? The system is not going to change just to accommodate Black people or anyone else for that matter. There is just way too much money to be made within the corrections industry and Americans want violent or repeat offenders locked up. Once you understand that simple fact, then you can start working on some real strategies. Of course, we all know that it is easier to blame the system, than to ask the offenders to change their ways!

I know that I said I'd stay away from too many statistics, but I must share these with you. Nearly one-third of the two million people in jails and prisons around the country will be released each year. That's over half a million criminals moving in and out of the system annually. And, guess what? According to the numbers, about eighty-five percent of them will re-offend within six months! (Remember my friend from the Chrysler 300?)

Here's a challenge for you: Instead of relying solely on statistics, take a look at the number of offenses that some of the people in prison have committed. Go to your local and state corrections web sites and you should be able to see why they are incarcerated. The wicked lie and connive and commit crimes. When they get caught, they become whiners, manipulators, and schemers. The softhearted and the uninitiated always fall for their sob stories while the rest of us clean up in the aftermath of their sociopathic and violent behavior. Not everyone can be a good citizen and some people belong behind bars. Maybe it's time we accept that fact and move forward.

I know that I've thrown a lot at you, but this is the real deal. If you were just curious about law enforcement then I hope you enjoyed the ride. For those of you looking to build a better relationship with your local law enforcement agency, now you know the truth. Don't worry, it's not as bad is it seems. Just follow the guidelines that I've laid out here and you'll be fine. If you have any questions, email me at dexterdiamond2000@yahoo.com and I'll be more than happy to help you any way that I can. Change is possible, but our communities must be willing to dig deeper for the truth, and realize that we have to make some changes too if we are going to be successful in fitting fully into this great American society.

"Only the supremely wise or the ignorant do not alter."

-CONFUCIUS

www.ingramcontent.com/pod-product-compliance
Lightning Source LLC
Chambersburg PA
CBHW052010280526
45793CB00005B/920